Come Light Our Hearts

General Intercessions for Ritual Celebrations,
Feast Days, and Civic Holidays

Come Light
Our Hearts

Neil J. Draves-Arpaia

ave maria press Notre Dame, IN

In memory of

Ms. M. Helen Doherty
(1912–1967)

Sr. Marie Louise Fournier, C.S.J.
(1910–1984)

Sr. Susanne Breckel, R.S.M., Ph.D.
(1925–1985)

Each prayerful,
each a timely mentor,
each an unforgettable teacher

© 1999 by Ave Maria Press, Inc.

All rights reserved. No part of this book may be used or reproduced in any manner whatsoever except in the case of reprints in the context of reviews, without written permission from Ave Maria Press, Inc., P.O. Box 428, Notre Dame, IN 46556.

International Standard Book Number: 0-87793-680-3

Cover and text design by Brian C. Conley

Printed and bound in the United States of America.

Library of Congress Cataloging-in-Publication Data
Draves-Arpaia, Neil J.
     Come light our hearts : general intercessions for ritual celebrations, feast days, and civic holidays / Neil J. Draves-Arpaia.
          p.   cm.
     ISBN 0-87793-680-3
     1. General intercessions—Catholic Church. 2. Fasts and feasts—Catholic Church. 3. Catholic Church—Liturgy Texts. I. Title.
BX2015.62.D72 1999
264'.027—dc21

                                              99-28693
                                              CIP

Contents

Part I
Ritual Celebrations

Baptism of Children

Reconciliation

First Eucharist

Confirmation

Marriage and Anniversaries

Mass for the Sick or Anointing

Funeral, Wake, or Memorial Service

Part II
Feasts and Memorials of Mary and the Saints

January

February

March

April

May

June

July

August

September

October

November

December

Masses of the Blessed Virgin Mary

Common of Saints

Part III
Special Circumstances

Part IV
Civic Holidays

Part V
Miscellaneous Petitions and Special Commemorations

Miscellaneous Petitions

Special Commemorations

Part VI
Litanies and Prayer Services

Introduction

The intercessions contained in this collection of prayers span a wide range of pastoral and liturgical circumstances outside of the Sunday and holy day masses or solemnities of the Lord. Many of the themes and concerns articulated in my previous book of intercessions, *Graciously Hear Us* (1998, Ave Maria Press), such as reverent living, care for the sick, justice for the economically poor, respect for life and creation, the conciliar call to holiness, support of human rights, and living the mysteries of faith in a Catholic tradition are also found in this collection. Wherever appropriate the petitions are universal in scope and invite the immediate assembly of believers to lend their voice in being of one mind and heart as they pray in union with the whole church.

The main focus in composing these intercessions is the praying assembly of Christian believers. In almost all liturgical celebrations the general intercessions bring the liturgy of the word to a close. The intercessions, therefore, are written to express the community's belief in the life-giving mystery of faith proclaimed at the table of God's word before continuing its celebration at the table of the eucharist. Not all liturgical celebrations include a Mass. This has been kept in mind especially for weddings, funerals, wakes, and reconciliation and other prayer services. The intercessions are formatted so that they can be easily adapted to special pastoral and liturgical circumstances. Where possible, options have been provided so as to accommodate various pastoral needs.

Unlike the intercessions in *Graciously Hear Us*, whose immediate inspiration was the assigned scriptural readings of the day and the liturgical season, these current intercessions are more thematic, since in many circumstances there are numerous options for scripture readings. At the same time, these petitions take up teachings and concerns articulated in sacred scripture. In most ritual Masses special focus is given to those who are receiving or celebrating a sacrament, have special need for the community's prayers, or are being commended to the love and compassion of God. In some places attention is given to the liturgical season in which a liturgy is being celebrated.

Civic holidays in the United States and Canada are treated with care so that the paschal mystery of Christ and the Christian life remain the center of the celebration. Intercessions written for special circumstances have been guided by the prayers and readings for Masses for Various Needs and Occasions from the Roman Sacramentary or from the directives found in the Order of Prayer in the Liturgy of the Hours and Celebration of the Eucharist.

Come Light Our Hearts includes intercessions for feasts and memorials of saints and secondary feasts of the Blessed Virgin Mary. Most of the solemnities, feasts, and obligatory memorials of saints each have their own general intercessions. Common formats for apostles, evangelists, martyrs, doctors, or any saint are included and may be used on the appropriate day. Optional memorials, based on the liturgical calendar for the United States and Canada, have only a single petition that can be easily integrated into one of the common formats. It should be noted that many of the petitions for memorials of saints were inspired by the heroic virtue of the particular saint, incidents in his or her life, and human and spiritual concerns under his or her patronage or to which he or she was dedicated. In the case of founders of religious orders, an optional intercession asking blessing upon that religious institute is included. The intercessions for liturgies celebrating the Mother of God are compatible with the themes found in the Collection of Masses of the BVM (1992).

Numerous miscellaneous petitions that can be integrated into the prayer of the faithful as circumstances arise can be found in Part V. The volume then concludes with prayer services that are intercessory in nature. These include litanies to the Holy Spirit suitable for assemblies, one of which is arranged as a nine-day preparatory prayer for Pentecost. Additionally, there is a commemoration of the dead and a prayer service appropriate for the end of the year.

May these general intercessions and prayers be helpful to pastors, homilists, liturgy planners, presiders, and most of all to God's people when, in one voice, they "confidently approach the throne of grace to receive mercy and favor and to find help in time of need" (Heb 4:16).

Using the Computer Disk

The accompanying computer disk has been included to make the petitions in this book even more accessible to you. By using this disk, you will be able to reproduce the petitions to meet your particular needs.

The files on this disk are saved in either Rich Text File (rtf) or DOS Text File (txt) format, sort of "generic" formats. In order to use this disk, you must have a computer and word processing software that allows you to access it. Either a Macintosh or Macintosh-compatible computer or an IBM or IBM-compatible computer using a Windows operating system will be able to open the files. If you have a Macintosh computer that is several years old, it may not be able to open the disk. Once the disk is opened, most word processing programs will then be able to access the information.

When using the disk, first open "Readme.txt." This document offers further instructions for opening the main text of *Come Light Our Hearts*. When working in a Windows environment, you will need to select the option "All Files" under the "List Files of Type" heading in the dialogue box. Unless you do this, the file may not appear.

Ritual Celebrations

Baptism, Easter Season (More Than One Child)

Option #1

[When the intercessions follow the baptism the presider's invitation should be adapted accordingly.]

Presider: Let us implore God to sustain the new life of grace in these children who (are to be/have been) reborn in these Easter waters and in all the baptized.

Petition Leader: Our response is: **"Pour out your Spirit, O God."**

Endow these children with every spiritual blessing. As we rejoice in Christ's resurrection, we pray:

Strengthen their families in love and peace. As we rejoice in Christ's resurrection, we pray:

Enable us to provide them with spiritual and moral guidance as they journey through life. As we rejoice in Christ's resurrection, we pray:

Safeguard them from all harm that they may advance in wisdom and grace. As we rejoice in Christ's resurrection, we pray:

Inspire them to live devoutly as members of the body of Christ. As we rejoice in Christ's resurrection, we pray:

Bestow on them the gift of prayer that their voices may be one with the church as it praises your redeeming love. As we rejoice in Christ's resurrection, we pray:

Sustain them by means of your Word and sacraments that they may arrive at the fullness of life when their earthly journey is complete. As we rejoice in Christ's resurrection, we pray:

Presider: Loving God, receive the prayers of this community as we invoke your Spirit on behalf of these children in the name of Christ, our risen Savior.

Baptism, Easter Season (More Than One Child)

Option #2

[When the intercessions follow the baptism the presider's invitation should be adapted accordingly.]

Presider: Let us call forth the life-giving Spirit on behalf of these children who (are to be/have been) reborn at the font of salvation and on all the baptized.

Petition Leader: Our response is: **"Loving God, send forth your Spirit."**

Through the power of your Spirit, the Giver of Life, may these children become a new creation in Christ, your Beloved. With joyful hearts, we pray:

Bestow the grace and peace of your Holy Spirit upon their parents and families to whom you have entrusted their life and well-being. With joyful hearts, we pray:

Surround them with the best of teachers in the ways of faith that they may advance in wisdom and truth as members of the body of Christ, the church. With joyful hearts, we pray:

Safeguard them always with your loving protection and deliver them from any physical or spiritual harm. With joyful hearts, we pray:

Bless them with the best of spiritual gifts in keeping with the glories of Christ, our risen Savior. With joyful hearts, we pray:

Strengthen us to be for them a community of praise and compassion sustained by the Word and sacraments of new life. With joyful hearts, we pray:

Set within their hearts the desire to be one with Christ in the reign of everlasting light. With joyful hearts, we pray:

Presider: God of all creation, receive our prayers on behalf of these children. By the power of your Holy Spirit help us to be instruments of your redeeming love in their lives. Grant our prayers in the name of Jesus, whose resurrection we proclaim now and forever.

Baptism, Outside of the Easter Season
(More Than One Child)

[When the intercessions follow the baptism the presider's invitation should be adapted accordingly.]

Presider: Let us pray on behalf of these children who (are to receive/have received) new life at the font of salvation and for the church as it journeys by the light of one faith and one baptism.

Petition Leader: Our response today is, **"God our life, hear us."**

We entrust to your loving care the life of these children. May your Holy Spirit sustain in them the grace of baptism all their days. We pray:

We ask for your blessing upon their parents and families. May the life of grace you bestow on these children flourish in peaceful surroundings. We pray:

We invoke your Spirit of truth to lead these children in pathways of justice and holiness. We pray:

We summon your Spirit to deepen within all Christians the grace of baptism. May our faith, hope, and love help to shape a life-giving future for these children. We pray:

We call upon your loving kindness to heal the wounds of sin and division among us. May the bonds of mutual care help us to be a faith-filled community of compassion. We pray:

We place our hope in your life-giving Word. May the dead who were sealed with the oil of gladness in baptism be in your company forever (especially _____). We pray:

Presider: God of tender mercy, you continuously offer us new life through the gospel of peace. Receive our prayers, especially for these children, and may your gift of the divine life of grace bring us to the joys of your reign. We ask this in the name of Jesus Christ, our Redeemer.

Baptism (More Than One Child, Litany Form A⁺)

[When the intercessions follow the baptism the presider's invitation should be adapted accordingly.]

Presider: Let us raise our voices in prayer on behalf of these children who (are to be/have been) reborn at the font of salvation.

Petition Leader: Our response today is: **"Graciously hear us, O God."**

Creating God, Source of Life, bless these children, we pray:

Redeeming God, Christ our Savior, give them your peace, we pray:

Indwelling God, Spirit of holiness, bestow on them the oil of gladness, we pray:

Sustaining God, Trinity of Love, guide and protect them, we pray:

Bless the lives of their parents, we pray:

Bestow on them all spiritual gifts, we pray:

Make them dedicated disciples, we pray:

Enrich the church through their faith, we pray:

Claim them for the reign of heaven, we pray:

Help them to grow in wisdom and grace, we pray:

Enable us to be for them signs of your love, we pray:

Safeguard them from all sin and harm, we pray:

Presider: Loving God, Trinity of Persons, accept our prayers for these children and by the power of your grace bring our baptismal faith to perfection, through Christ, our Lord.

⁺These petitions are designed to be read as a litany. The proclamation should move quickly but not in a rushed or hurried manner.

Baptism (More Than One Child, Litany Form B)

[This format anticipates the baptism and includes the invocation of the saints and prayer of exorcism.[+]]

Presider: Let us raise our voices in prayer on behalf of these children who are to be reborn at the font of salvation.

Petition Leader: Our response today is: **"Graciously hear us, O God."**

Creating God, Source of Life, bless these children, we pray:

Redeeming God, Christ our Savior, give them your peace, we pray:

Indwelling God, Spirit of holiness, bestow on them the oil of gladness, we pray:

Sustaining God, Trinity of Love, guide and protect them, we pray:

Bless the lives of their parents, we pray:

Bestow on them all spiritual gifts, we pray:

Make them dedicated disciples, we pray:

Enrich the church through their faith, we pray:

Claim them for the reign of heaven, we pray:

Help them to grow in wisdom and grace, we pray:

Enable us to be for them signs of your love, we pray:

Safeguard them from all sin and harm, we pray:

Presider (or Petition Leader): Let us invoke the saints to pray for us.
Holy Mary, Mother of God . . . **pray for us,**
St. Joseph . . . **pray for us,**
St. John the Baptist . . . **pray for us,**
St. Mary Magdalene . . . **pray for us,**
Holy Prophets of God . . . **pray for us,**
Holy Patriarchs and Matriarchs . . . **pray for us,**

Holy Apostles of God . . . **pray for us,**
Holy Martyrs of God . . . **pray for us,**
[Names of any patronal saints may be added]
All holy women and men of God . . . **pray for us.**

[The presider may conclude the litany with one of the prayers for exorcism as provided in the Roman ritual or with the following:]

Loving God, Trinity of Persons, accept our prayers for these children, and by the power of your grace bring our baptismal faith to perfection, through Christ, our Lord.

---

†These petitions are designed to be read as a litany. The proclamation should move quickly but not in a rushed or hurried manner.

Baptism, Easter Season (One Child)
Option #1

[When the intercessions follow the baptism the presider's invitation should be adapted accordingly.]

Presider: Let us implore God to sustain the new life of grace in this child who (is to be/has been) reborn in these Easter waters and in all the baptized.

Petition Leader: Our response is: **"Pour out your Spirit, O God."**

Endow this child with every spiritual blessing. As we rejoice in Christ's resurrection, we pray:

Strengthen his/her family in love and peace. As we rejoice in Christ's resurrection, we pray:

Enable us to provide this child with spiritual and moral guidance as he/she journeys through life. As we rejoice in Christ's resurrection, we pray:

Safeguard him/her from all harm that he/she may advance in wisdom and grace. As we rejoice in Christ's resurrection, we pray:

Inspire him/her to live devoutly as a member of the body of Christ. As we rejoice in Christ's resurrection, we pray:

Bestow on him/her the gift of prayer that his/her voice may be one with the church as it praises your redeeming love. As we rejoice in Christ's resurrection, we pray:

Sustain him/her by means of your Word and sacraments that he/she may arrive at the fullness of life when his/her earthly journey is complete. As we rejoice in Christ's resurrection, we pray:

Presider: Loving God, receive the prayers of this community as we invoke your Spirit on behalf of this child in the name of Christ, our risen Savior.

Baptism, Easter Season (One Child)
Option #2

[When the intercessions follow the baptism the presider's invitation should be adapted accordingly.]

Presider: Let us call forth the life-giving Spirit on behalf of this child who (is to be/has been) reborn at the font of salvation.

Petition Leader: Our response is: **"Loving God, send forth your Spirit."**

Through the power of your Spirit, the Giver of Life, may this child become a new creation in Christ, your Beloved. With joyful hearts, we pray:

Bestow the grace and peace of your Holy Spirit upon his/her parents and family to whom you have entrusted his/her life and well-being. With joyful hearts, we pray:

Surround him/her with the best of teachers in the ways of faith that he/she may advance in wisdom and truth as a member of the body of Christ, the church. With joyful hearts, we pray:

Safeguard him/her always with your loving protection and deliver him/her from any physical or spiritual harm. With joyful hearts, we pray:

Bless him/her with the best of spiritual gifts in keeping with the glories of Christ, our risen savior. With joyful hearts, we pray:

Strengthen us to be for him/her a community of praise and compassion sustained by the Word and sacraments of new life. With joyful hearts, we pray:

Set within his/her heart the desire to be one with Christ in the reign of everlasting light. With joyful hearts, we pray:

Presider: God of all creation, receive our prayers on behalf of this child. By the power of your Holy Spirit help us to be instruments of your redeeming love in his/her life. Grant our prayers in the name of Jesus, whose resurrection we proclaim now and forever.

Baptism, Outside of the Easter Season (One Child)

[When the intercessions follow the baptism the presider's invitation should be adapted accordingly.]

Presider: Let us pray on behalf of this child who (is to receive/has received) new life at the font of salvation and for the church as it journeys by the light of one faith and one baptism.

Petition Leader: Our response today is, **"God our life, hear us."**

We entrust to your loving care the life of this child. May your Holy Spirit sustain in him/her the grace of baptism through every season of life. We pray:

We ask for your blessing upon his/her parents and family. May the life of grace you bestow on this child flourish in peaceful surroundings. We pray:

We invoke your Spirit of truth to lead this child in pathways of justice and holiness. We pray:

We summon your Spirit to deepen within all Christians the grace of baptism. May our faith, hope, and love help to shape a life-giving future for this child. We pray:

We call upon your loving kindness to heal the wounds of sin and division among us. May the bonds of mutual care help us to be a faith-filled community of compassion. We pray:

We place our hope in your life-giving Word. May the dead who were sealed with the oil of gladness in baptism be in your company forever (especially _____). We pray:

Presider: God of tender mercy, you continuously offer us new life through the gospel of peace. Receive our prayers, especially for this child, and may your gift of the divine life of grace bring us to the joys of your reign. We ask this in the name of Jesus Christ, our Redeemer.

Baptism (One Child, Litany Form A[+])

[When the intercessions follow the baptism the presider's invitation should be adapted accordingly.]

Presider: Let us raise our voices in prayer on behalf of this child who (is to be/has been) reborn at the font of salvation.

Petition Leader: Our response today is: **"Graciously hear us, O God."**

Creating God, Source of Life, bless this child, we pray:

Redeeming God, Christ our Savior, give him/her your peace, we pray:

Indwelling God, Spirit of holiness, bestow on him/her the oil of gladness, we pray:

Sustaining God, Trinity of Love, guide and protect him/her, we pray:

Bless the lives of his/her parents, we pray:

Bestow on him/her all spiritual gifts, we pray:

Make him/her a dedicated disciple, we pray:

Enrich the church through his/her faith, we pray:

Claim him/her for the reign of heaven, we pray:

Help him/her to grow in wisdom and grace, we pray:

Enable us to be for him/her signs of your love, we pray:

Safeguard him/her from all sin and harm, we pray:

Presider: Loving God, Trinity of Persons, accept our prayers for this child, and by the power of your grace bring our baptismal faith to perfection, through Christ, our Lord.

[+]These petitions are designed to be read as a litany. The proclamation should move quickly but not in a rushed or hurried manner.

Baptism (One Child, Litany Form B)

[This format anticipates the baptism and includes the invocation of the saints and prayer of exorcism.+]

Presider: Let us raise our voices in prayer on behalf of this child who is to be reborn at the font of salvation.

Petition Leader: Our response today is: **"Graciously hear us, O God."**

Creating God, Source of Life, bless this child, we pray:

Redeeming God, Christ our Savior, give him/her your peace, we pray:

Indwelling God, Spirit of holiness, bestow on him/her the oil of gladness, we pray:

Sustaining God, Trinity of Love, guide and protect him/her, we pray:

Bless the lives of his/her parents, we pray:

Bestow on him/her all spiritual gifts, we pray:

Make him/her a dedicated disciple, we pray:

Enrich the church through his/her faith, we pray:

Claim him/her for the reign of heaven, we pray:

Help him/her to grow in wisdom and grace, we pray:

Enable us to be for him/her signs of your love, we pray:

Safeguard him/her from all sin and harm, we pray:

Presider (or Petition Leader): Let us invoke the saints to pray for us.
Holy Mary, Mother of God . . . **pray for us,**
St. Joseph . . . **pray for us,**
St. John the Baptist . . . **pray for us,**
St. Mary Magdalene . . . **pray for us,**
Holy Prophets of God . . . **pray for us,**
Holy Patriarchs and Matriarchs . . . **pray for us,**

Holy Apostles of God . . . **pray for us**,
Holy Martyrs of God . . . **pray for us**,
[Names of any patronal saints may be added]
All holy women and men of God . . . **pray for us**,

[The presider may conclude the litany with one of the prayers for exorcism as provided in the Roman ritual or with the following:]

Loving God, Trinity of Persons, accept our prayers for this child, and by the power of your grace bring our baptismal faith to perfection, through Christ, our Lord.

---

†These petitions are designed to be read as a litany. The proclamation should move quickly but not in a rushed or hurried manner.

First Reconciliation (Children)

[The following is a penitential litany that may be led by children as part of a celebration of first reconciliation.]

Presider: Jesus taught that God forgives our sins when we tell God we are sorry. Because we believe the things Jesus taught, we pray that God will forgive our sins.

Petition Leader: Our prayer response is, **"God in heaven, we are sorry for our sins."**

Jesus taught us to love God. For the times we have failed to do what is right in God's sight, we pray:

Jesus taught us to love our neighbor. For the times we have been hurtful to others, we pray:

Jesus taught us to be kind to others. For the times we have been selfish, we pray:

Jesus taught us that God loves us always. For the times we have failed to thank God for loving us, we pray:

Jesus taught that God is forgiving. For the times we have failed to forgive others when they are sorry for hurting us, we pray:

Jesus taught us to respect all the things God has made. For the times we have not acted with care and respect, we pray:

[The litany may conclude with the Lord's Prayer or some other penitential prayer suitable for children, or with the following presider prayer.]

Presider: God, by dying for us on the cross, Jesus has shown how much you love us and forgive our sins. With the help of your grace may we do all that Jesus taught by his words and actions. We ask this in Jesus' name.

Communal Reconciliation (Youth and Young Adults)

[The following intercessions are penitential in nature and may be used as part of a reconciliation service. Extra intercessions have been included so as to provide options for liturgy planners. Those that are appropriate to the age and circumstances of the assembly should be selected. The petitions may be offered by more than one leader.]

Presider: By word and example, Christ taught us to love God and neighbor. Let us seek God's forgiveness for the times we have failed to take Christ's teachings to heart.

Petition Leader: Our response to each intercession is, **"God in heaven, have mercy on us."**

For the times we have disregarded God's commands, we turn to God and ask:

For the times we have failed to give God glory by withholding our public praise and worship, we turn to God and ask:

For the times we have failed to honor God's name or have shown disrespect for the name of Jesus, we turn to God and ask:

For the times we have withheld proper respect for persons in authority, particularly our parents, we turn to God and ask:

For the times we have shown contempt for the rights of others, especially toward their possessions or physical safety, we turn to God and ask:

For the times we have acted with cruelty toward others, especially other family members, we turn to God and ask:

For the times we have held on to our anger and resentment instead of acting with forgiveness, we turn to God and ask:

For the times we have shown disregard for our personal health through the abuse of drugs, alcohol, or food, we turn to God and ask:

For the times we have failed to be chaste in our behavior, we turn to God and ask:

[The litany may conclude with the Lord's Prayer or some other penitential prayer, or with the following presider's prayer.]

Presider: Merciful God, hear us as we call on your forgiving love. With the help of your grace may we live better lives that are pleasing in your sight. We ask this in the name of Jesus.

Communal Reconciliation (Adults)

Option #1

[The following litany is penitential in nature and may be used as part of a communal reconciliation service.]

Presider: Let us implore the God of infinite goodness and compassion to look kindly on us.
[Pause for silent prayer.]

Presider: Turn with mercy toward us, O God!

All: Have mercy on us in your goodness!

Presider: When we have failed as disciples of Christ to bear our share of the hardship in witnessing to the gospel of compassion.

All: Have mercy on us in your goodness!

Presider: When we have failed in hope by loving the passing things of earth more than the everlasting life of heaven.

All: Have mercy on us in your goodness!

Presider: When we have failed to trust that your love would see us through turbulent times.

All: Have mercy on us in your goodness!

Presider: When we have failed to accept your pardon and peace by clinging to our guilt and shame.

All: Have mercy on us in your goodness!

Presider: When our love failed to do justice for the poor and oppressed, and instead we gave priority to our selfish concerns.

All: Have mercy on us in your goodness!

Presider: When we have allowed our anger to turn into rage, our rage into violence against life and place all blame on you.

All: Have mercy on us in your goodness!

Presider: Mindful of God's immense love for us, let us pray as Jesus taught, Our Father . . .

Redeeming God, continue to free us from the moorings of sinfulness! Deliver us through a new exodus of grace and peace, that our true liberation will be a humanity sanctified to share your life, O Trinity of Persons! Grant this through Christ, our Lord.

Communal Reconciliation (Adults)

Option #2

[The following penitential litany is based on the theme of covenant as expressed in the Magnificat, Luke 1:46-55. It may be included in a communal reconciliation service during the Advent season.]

Presider: Like our ancestors in faith, let us be mindful of God's ageless mercy and pray to be renewed in God's grace and peace.

Petition Leader: God, in the greatness of your love you have established an everlasting covenant with us in Christ. Forgive us for the times we have failed to uphold its commands to love you and our neighbor. Lord, have mercy.
Assembly: Lord, have mercy.

God, you who are mighty have done great things for us. Forgive our sin of failing to offer you fitting praise and thanks. Lord, have mercy.
Assembly: Lord, have mercy.

God, your mercy is from generation to generation. Forgive us for our failure to act mercifully toward those who have offended us. Lord, have mercy.
Assembly: Lord, have mercy.

God, you have cast away the arrogant and conceited. Forgive our sins of pride and for failing to walk humbly in your presence. Lord, have mercy.
Assembly: Lord, have mercy.

God, you have lifted up the lowly to high places. Forgive us for failing in the requirements of justice for the poor of our world. Lord, have mercy.
Assembly: Lord, have mercy.

God, you have filled the hungry with good things. Forgive our selfishness and greed, especially the times we have withheld our bread from the hungry. Lord, have mercy.
Assembly: Lord, have mercy.

God, you have come to our aid for you are rich in mercy. Forgive our sins of omission, especially when we have failed to aid our neighbor in need. Lord, have mercy.
Assembly: Lord, have mercy.

[The Lord's Prayer may follow and the litany concludes with the presider's prayer.]

Presider: Let us ask God to forgive our sins, praying as Jesus taught, Our Father . . .

Loving God, we look to your covenant of mercy for new life. Hear our prayers and grant us pardon and peace. We ask this in Jesus' name.

Communal Reconciliation (Adults)
Option #3

[The following penitential litany is based on the Judgment of the Nations, Matthew 25:31-46. It may be included in a communal reconciliation especially during the Lenten season.]

Presider: Let us invoke the mercy of God for the times we have failed to act justly and compassionately as the gospel commands.

Petition Leader: God, you have filled us with good things and fed us with the best of wheat. For the times we have failed to share our bread with the hungry and acted selfishly we pray, Lord, have mercy.
Assembly: Lord, have mercy.

God, you gave us your Spirit to quench our thirst for holiness. For the times we have ignored the prompting of your Spirit to help those who thirst for justice in our world we pray, Christ, have mercy.
Assembly: Christ, have mercy.

God, you have welcomed us into the household of Christ through baptism. For the times we have failed to show your hospitality to strangers and those in need we pray, Lord, have mercy.
Assembly: Lord, have mercy.

God, in Christ you have clothed us with a mantle of salvation. For the times we have failed to clothe the poor among us with dignity and respect we pray, Christ, have mercy.
Assembly: Christ, have mercy.

God, you have bestowed on us healing and peace through the saving death of Christ. For the times we have failed to be a healing presence in the lives of others we pray, Lord, have mercy.
Assembly: Lord, have mercy.

God, you have freed us from slavery to sin and death. For the times we have dismissed the cries of those unjustly deprived of liberty we pray, Christ, have mercy.
Assembly: Christ, have mercy.

God, you have called us in Christ to be compassionate as you are compassionate. For the times we have been instruments of rancor and division rather than instruments of your loving kindness we pray, Lord, have mercy.

Assembly: Lord, have mercy.

God, you have lavished us with love in Christ and raised us up. For the times we have failed to express our gratitude and love for you we pray, Christ, have mercy.

Assembly: Christ, have mercy.

God, in Christ you have revealed to us the fullness of your saving word. For the times we have disbelieved the gospel of peace and mercy we pray, Lord, have mercy.

Assembly: Lord, have mercy.

[The Lord's Prayer may follow and the intercessions conclude with the presider's prayer.]

Presider: Let us praise God's loving kindness in the words Jesus gave us, Our Father . . .

God, ever rich in mercy, hear our prayers for your pardon and peace. Renew us in your love and by the power of your Spirit help us to live as disciples of the compassionate Christ, who lives and reigns with you and the Holy Spirit, one God forever and ever.

First Eucharist (Mass for Children in the Easter Season)
Option #1

Presider: The friends of Jesus were filled with happiness because God raised him from the dead. Jesus told his followers to remember his love whenever they came together and to give thanks to God. So, we pray to be thankful for God's many gifts.

Petition Leader: Our response today is, **"God, hear our prayer."**

God, you sent us Jesus to be our light. We thank you for the light of our faith and ask you to be with us always. We pray:

God, you gave us Jesus to be our Bread of Life. We thank you for inviting us to celebrate Jesus' love in this holy meal. We pray:

God, you blessed us in baptism with the Holy Spirit. We thank you for the gift of new life and ask for the Spirit's help in all we do. We pray:

God, you are the Creator of all people. We thank you for our family and friends and ask you to bless our world with peace. We pray:

God, you taught us through Jesus to love one another. We thank you for those who show us how to follow Jesus, especially our parents, teachers, and church leaders. We pray:

God, you filled Jesus with love for persons who were sick and in need of healing. We thank you for those who care for us when we are ill or sad and ask you to help those who are not well. We pray:

God, you taught us through Jesus that one day your friends would celebrate your love in heaven. We thank you for this good news and trust that our relatives and friends who have died are safe in your care. We pray:

Presider: Loving God, our hearts are filled with joy because you love us. We ask you to receive our prayers through Jesus, who taught us to love you in return.

First Eucharist (Mass for Children in the Easter Season)
Option #2

Presider: Jesus rose from the dead and prays for us. Let us ask Jesus to be with us on this special day.

Petition Leader: Our response is, **"Jesus, be with us!"**

Jesus, we believe you are the Son of God. May all who are God's children by baptism be filled with your Spirit. We pray:

Jesus, you called people to follow you. May we do what pleases you at home, in school, and at play. We pray:

Jesus, you invited your friends together to hear the good news. May we listen to your Word that teaches us to be holy. We pray:

Jesus, you shared a final meal with your friends before you died. May we who share your body and blood for the first time be counted as your friends. We pray:

Jesus, you rose from the dead and your friends were filled with joy. May our families be blessed with happiness knowing that you are always with us in Spirit. We pray:

Jesus, you promised to be with those who need God's special care. May people who are sick or sad know you are there to help them, especially through the kindness of other people. We pray:

Jesus, you show us the way to God. May your love bring our relatives and friends who have died into the joy of heaven. We pray:

Presider: God, Jesus promised to pray for us in your presence. Hear our prayers through Jesus, our Savior and brother, who lives with you and the Holy Spirit forever.

First Eucharist
(Mass for Children Outside of the Easter Season)

Presider: Jesus taught his friends to pray and to ask for God's help. On this special day let us pray for our first communicants and the good of other people.

Petition Leader: Our response today is, **"God, hear our prayer."**

Bless all our church leaders with the Holy Spirit that they may help Christians to be a people of peace and goodness. We pray:

Bless each of us who share the body and blood of Christ for the first time that we may live as Jesus taught. We pray:

Bless our parents and friends with good health and true love for their neighbors. We pray:

Bless the leaders of our country and our cities so that all people may live in peace. We pray:

Bless those who protect us, especially police officers and firefighters, that they may be safe as they help others. We pray:

Bless all the sick and those who care for them, especially doctors and nurses. We pray:

Bless those who are hungry, especially children and infants, and show us how to be more helpful to them. We pray:

Bless those who work to keep our planet healthy, and teach us to treat the earth with respect. We pray:

Bless our relatives and friends who have died with eternal life (especially _____). We pray:

Presider: God, hear our prayers and fill us with every blessing on this special day in the name of Jesus.

First Eucharist (Young Adults)

Presider: God's love draws us together to be alive in Christ. Let us call upon God's love especially for those who are about to receive the eucharist for the first time.

Petition Leader: Our response today is, **"May your love be with us."**

We ask for the blessing of unity and peace for the church that it may be strengthened by the word of God and the sacraments of life. Confidently we pray to our God:

We implore God's Spirit to bless those who share in the eucharist for the first time with the grace and peace of the risen Christ. Confidently we pray to our God:

We ask God to surround these first communicants with persons deeply committed to the gospel of Jesus Christ and the good of all humankind. Confidently we pray to our God:

We entrust them to the guidance of the Holy Spirit that they may be led to deeper intimacy with the risen Christ and endowed with every spiritual gift. Confidently we pray to our God:

We summon the Spirit of reconciliation and healing to abide within every human heart that all peoples may enjoy the blessing of friendship and community. Confidently we pray to our God:

We call upon the consoling love of Christ to sustain those who are ill or afflicted in any way. Confidently we pray to our God:

We entrust to God's tender mercies those who have died, especially the relatives and friends of each of us gathered here today. Confidently we pray to our God:

Presider: Kind and loving God, accept the prayers of your church, and by the Spirit's power open our hearts to receive the Word and Bread of new life who is Jesus Christ, our Savior.

Confirmation (Youth)

[These petitions are written to be led by a member of the confirmation group.]

Presider: God is the giver of every good gift. Let us nourish God's gifts with prayer.

Petition Leader: Our response to each petition is, **"Loving God, hear our prayer."**

God has given us the gift of life. May we always defend life in the Spirit of Jesus. We pray:

God has given us a new birth through baptism and the Holy Spirit. May we cherish the gift of our faith and act on it. We pray:

God has given us the gift of a faith community. May we share our gifts and talents within our parish families for the good of the church. We pray:

God has been generous in loving us. May we be generous in our love for God and neighbor. We pray:

God has given the world the gift of salvation in Christ. May all nations live in the peace of the Lord. We pray:

God has given us the gift of creation. May we grow in our respect for our natural resources so that all people may enjoy the beauty of the earth. We pray:

God's gifts of love are given to us through Christ. May the Holy Spirit help us to be instruments of Christ's peace in our homes and among our friends. We pray:

God bestows on each person special gifts and abilities. May the Spirit of Christ help us to act responsibly by developing our hearts and minds by the light of truth. We pray:

God has created us to be a part of the human family. May we show kindness and care for others, especially any who are sick and suffering. We pray:

Presider: God in heaven, through the gift of your Holy Spirit you bring peace and joy to our lives. Hear our prayers and keep us strong in faith, hope, and love all our days. We ask this through Christ, our Lord.

Confirmation (Young Adults)
Option #1

Presider: Let us raise our voices in prayer, calling upon God to bestow all grace and peace upon the church and those to be confirmed.

Petition Leader: Our response is, **"Give us your grace, O God."**

[If the petitions are led by a confirmation candidate, the following should be adapted to read "us" or "our" rather than "them" or "their."]

God of light, bless and keep the church vibrant in faith, hope, and love, we pray:

God of peace, uphold in those to be confirmed a love for Christ and the church, we pray:

God of life, sustain in these youths the grace of baptism, we pray:

God of mercy, by your Spirit give them the gift of compassion, we pray:

God of love, strengthen them to be strong advocates of life, we pray:

God of life, bestow on them the oil of gladness and the mantle of justice, we pray:

God of all creation, endow them with every spiritual blessing and the desire to be united to you, we pray:

God of holiness, protect them from all evil as they journey through life, we pray:

God of perfect wisdom, enlighten their hearts and minds to the wonders of your truth, we pray:

God of the living and the dead, bring all your faithful people to the banquet of eternal life, we pray:

Presider: Loving God, Trinity of Persons, hear our prayers and sustain in us the joy of salvation through Christ, our Savior and the Spirit's power.

Confirmation (Young Adults)
Option #2

Presider: Let us intercede on behalf of those confirmed today asking God to bestow on them the Holy Spirit's gifts of faithfulness and love.

Petition Leader: Our prayer response is, **"Lord, give us your grace."**

[It is encouraged that a member of the confirmation group lead these petitions.]

Send forth the Spirit of wisdom to lead us in the way of truth and goodness. We ask in faith:

Pour into our hearts the Spirit of understanding to enlighten us as we strive to follow Christ and live by his Word. We ask in faith:

Give us your Spirit of good counsel that we may be blessed in the choices we make throughout life's journey. We ask in faith:

Sustain in us your strengthening Spirit to guide us in times of trial, hardship, and uncertainty. We ask in faith:

Uphold us by the Holy Spirit that we may live reverently and promote respect for the life of others, for all creation, and for our own spiritual well-being. We ask in faith:

Through the Spirit of unity endow us with the gift of prayer that we may be attentive to your voice and praise your goodness as members of the body of Christ, the church. We ask in faith:

Presider: Gracious God, source of every good gift, send the Spirit, the Giver of Life, into the hearts of your people so that all we ask for may be inspired by your love for us in Christ, our Lord.

Confirmation (Adults)

Presider: Drawing on the strength of our baptismal faith, let us pray for one another and for the good of the church.

Petition Leader: Our response is, **"God of love, hear our prayer."**

God, send forth the light of wisdom that your people may be sustained by the truth of your Word. We ask in faith:

God, send forth the creating Spirit to nourish the church, the body of Christ, with every blessing. We ask in faith:

God, send forth the Spirit of unity that the church may walk by the light of one faith and one baptism. We ask in faith:

God, send forth the Giver of Life, that all nations may live reverently in your sight. We ask in faith:

God, send forth the power of your love that all creation may be renewed in the peace of Christ. We ask in faith:

God, send forth the Spirit of peace that those confirmed this day may advance in the ways of justice and holiness. We ask in faith:

God, send forth the enlightening Spirit to guide these believers as they journey through life. We ask in faith:

God, send forth the consoling Spirit to be our helper and friend in time of trial and uncertainty. We ask in faith:

Presider: God, Giver of all good gifts, hear the prayers of your people and by the Spirit's grace fashion us to be united to Christ in his mission of mercy and peace. Grant this through Christ, our Redeemer.

Marriage
Option #1

Presider: Having witnessed [*Name and Name's*] vows, let us pray for them and for one another.

Petition Leader: Our response to each intercession is: **"God of love, hear our prayer."**

For [*Name and Name*] as they begin their vowed life as husband and wife, may they be blessed by God's grace and peace, we pray:

For the home which they will build together, may it be a dwelling place of Christ's love in the Spirit, we pray:

For their families and relatives who have brought them to this day, may each of their loved ones be blessed with good health and happiness, we pray:

For married persons, may the mutual love of spouses be a source of strength for families and society, we pray:

For single persons, widowed men and women, may each find in caring relatives and friendships personal joy and love, we pray:

For each of us gathered here today to share in [*Name and Name's*] joy, may the word of God continue to inspire all of us to make a better world built on love and peace, we pray:

For troubled marriages and for any who are struggling to heal from divorce, may the Spirit of Jesus bring a rebirth of love and strength, we pray:

Presider: God of love and mercy, receive our prayers on this joyous occasion and keep your Spirit of love and fidelity alive in our hearts. Grant this through Christ, our Lord.

Marriage
Option #2

Presider: Through prayer let us call upon God's loving kindness for [*Name and Name*] and for the good of all peoples.

Petition Leader: Our response to each petition is, **"Uphold us in your love, O God."**

For [*Name and Name*] at the beginning of their married life, may the sacrament of their love be a sign of God's goodness among us. We ask in faith:

For the home which their love creates, may it be a place of welcome filled with the spirit of Christian hospitality. We ask in faith:

For their families and friends, may all who are dear to them be surrounded by God's tender care. We ask in faith:

For all married persons, may the mutual love of husband and wife be an instrument of God's peace to strengthen families and society. We ask in faith:

For any who are struggling in their marriage, may the Spirit of God foster healing and a rebirth of love. We ask in faith:

For each of us who has gathered to rejoice with [*Name and Name*], may God's word in its richness inspire us to live reverently and peaceably with all creation. We ask in faith:

[When marriage takes place within Mass the following petition may be included:]
For all who draw near to share the one bread and one cup of blessing in this celebration, may Christ's sacramental presence deepen our bonds of unity. We ask in faith:

For our beloved dead (especially _____ [the names of deceased persons significant to the couple may be included here]), may God's loving kindness bid them welcome into the wedding feast of heaven. We ask in faith:

Presider: Good and gracious God, receive our prayers, and may the Spirit of Christ abide among us to your honor and glory. Grant our prayers through Jesus Christ, our Savior.

Marriage
Option #3

Presider: Let us join our voices in prayer with [*Name and Name*] as they call upon God's grace and peace.

Petition Leader: Our prayer response to each petition is, **"God, may your love abide in us."**

We entrust to your care [*Name and Name*], whom you made your own in baptism. May your gift of Christian faith strengthen their resolve to live as husband and wife. Trusting in your goodness, we pray:

We call upon your loving kindness to accompany this newly married couple as they journey through life together. May the Spirit of wisdom inspire them to love tenderly and to act justly. Trusting in your goodness, we pray:

We look to your Word to show us the path of life. May the good news of Jesus Christ find a dwelling place in the hearts of all believers. Trusting in your goodness, we pray:

We ask for the blessings of good health and happiness for all who are dear to [*Name and Name*]. May their families and friends experience your loving kindness daily. Trusting in your goodness, we pray:

We invoke your Holy Spirit to accompany engaged couples, the widowed, and single persons. May your grace sustain all people of good will. Trusting in your goodness, we pray:

[When marriage is celebrated within Mass the following petition may be included:]
We look to your Spirit to sustain the church in unity in peace. May all who share in the body and blood of Christ this day be fortified in faith, hope, and love. Trusting in your goodness, we pray:

We call upon your tender mercy to welcome into the wedding feast of heaven all who died believing in you (especially _____ [the names of deceased persons significant to the couple may be included here]). May we be consoled by the hope of eternal life. Trusting in your goodness, we pray:

Presider: God, ever rich in compassion, in faith we look to your goodness to enrich our lives. Hear our prayers, which we place before you in the name of Jesus Christ, our Redeemer.

Marriage
Option #4

Presider: [*Name and Name*] have sealed the sacrament of their love through Christian marriage. Let us join our voices in prayer as we call upon God to be with them on life's journey.

Petition Leader: Our response to each petition is, **"God, graciously hear us."**

We look to your love to sustain [*Name and Name*] in their promise to love and honor each other all their days. Bring their resolve to perfection in you. O God, hear us:

We remember that your loving kindness has renewed all creation in Christ. May [*Name and Name*] continue to draw new life from their consecration in the Lord. O God, hear us:

We celebrate Christ's love for the church, his body. May this mystery of faith empower [*Name and Name*] to follow the way of self-giving love as Christian husband and wife. O God, hear us:

We praise the wonder of your mercy that invites us to love you. May all people of good will be attentive to your Spirit calling us to love tenderly and to act with kindness toward others. O God, hear us:

We entrust our families and friends to your constant care. May our loved ones be blessed with your loving protection all their days. O God, hear us:

We place before you any who are ill and in need of healing. May your love renew the sick in body, mind, and spirit. O God, hear us:

[When marriage is celebrated within Mass the following petition may be included:]
We gather at table to celebrate the wedding feast of the Lamb of God. May our sharing in the body and blood of Christ fill us with longing for the good things of heaven. O God, hear us:

Presider: God, in your loving kindness hear our prayers and by your Spirit bring to completion the work of love you have begun in [*Name and Name*]. Grant our prayer through Christ, our Lord.

Marriage (Special Circumstances)
Option #1

[The following intercessions are suitable in "disparity of cult" circumstances.]

Presider: Let us join with [*Name and Name*] in praying for their marriage, their families, our faith community, and world.

Petition Leader: Please respond to each intercession by asking: **"Spirit of love, dwell in us."**

For [*Name and Name*] as they begin their marriage, may God be glorified in them and our world be happier because of their committed love. We pray to God:

For their families, may those who are dear to them be blessed with God's loving protection. We pray to God:

For all married persons, may the mutual love and respect of husband and wife create homes where compassion, understanding, and care abound. We pray to God:

For those engaged to be married, may God inspire those approaching marriage to seek self-giving love as the greatest of gifts in this life. We pray to God:

For widows and widowers and all who experience the loss of a loved one, may God's Spirit console the sorrowing and give them renewed strength as they continue life's journey. We pray to God:

For our faith communities, may God's Spirit fill each human heart with a desire to know and worship the One God and Creator of all humankind. We pray to God:

For our world, may God's wisdom and peace be with national leaders, and may each person of good will help build a world committed to peace and justice for all. We pray to God:

For the personal needs and concerns each of us carry within us. Let us pray in the quiet of our hearts. [Petition leader, please allow for a sufficient pause before concluding.] We pray to God:

[The Lord's Prayer may follow when Mass is not celebrated. The presider extends the invitation to pray in the words Jesus gave us: "Our Father . . ."]

Presider: God our Creator, you are known by so many names and yet the most suitable of all is God of love. Hear us as we call upon you to abide among us in Spirit. Sustain this newly married couple throughout their lives and bring to completion the good you have begun in them. We pray in the strength of our faith. [or, *We pray in the name of Jesus.*]

Marriage (Special Circumstances)
Option #2

[The following intercessions are suitable for an older Christian couple, a second marriage, or convalidation between two baptized persons.]

Presider: Now that you have sealed your love in the covenant of marriage, let us invoke God's help and strength that you may live this sacrament in mutual fidelity and respect.

Petition Leader: Our response is, **"God of love, give us your grace."**

By the working of the Holy Spirit may you grow rich in your love for God, for each other, and for all who are dear to you. Rejoicing in Christ's love for the church, we pray:

By the grace of the sacraments may the mystery of Christ in you lead to a holy and blameless life. Rejoicing in Christ's love for the church, we pray:

By your commitment to live reverently and respectfully as husband and wife may the church and society be enriched in every way. Rejoicing in Christ's love for the church, we pray:

By your readiness to care for each other in good times and bad may you be instruments of peace and compassion in each other's life. Rejoicing in Christ's love for the church, we pray:

By your hope in the gospel's promise of eternal life may you set your hearts on the greater gifts that lead to the wedding feast of heaven. Rejoicing in Christ's love for the church, we pray:

[If the celebration of eucharist does not follow and the nuptial blessing is omitted, the presider may immediately invite those present to pray the Lord's Prayer. The rite would conclude with the following prayer and a simple blessing taken from the Roman Rite of Marriage. When a nuptial blessing is used the presider may incorporate it into the general intercessions so that they are harmonious but not a duplication. The following concluding prayer would be omitted.]

Presider: Kind and loving God, Creator of the universe, through the saving mystery of Christ, the wedding feast of the Lamb has begun. Hear our prayers for [*Name and Name*]. Strengthen them with your grace and bring to completion the good you have begun in them. Grant this through Christ, our Lord.

Marriage (Special Circumstances)
Option #3

[The following intercessions are suitable for a marriage between a Catholic and unbaptized person, especially an older couple, a second marriage, or convalidation.]

Presider: Now that you have sealed your love in the covenant of marriage, let us invoke God's help and strength that you may live in mutual fidelity and respect.

Petition Leader: Our response is, **"God of love, give us your grace."**

By the working of the Holy Spirit may you grow rich in your love for God, for each other, and for all who are dear to you. Rejoicing in God's love for all peoples, we pray:

By your commitment to live reverently and respectfully as husband and wife may our faith communities and society be enriched in every way. Rejoicing in God's love for all peoples, we pray:

By your readiness to care for each other in good times and bad may you be instruments of peace and compassion in each other's life. Rejoicing in God's love for all peoples, we pray:

By your dedication to creating a home together may your hospitality extend to any who come to you in time of need. Rejoicing in God's love for all peoples, we pray:

By the grace of God may you learn to value the things that really matter so that when your life on earth is complete you will be found rich in a harvest of justice. Rejoicing in God's love for all peoples, we pray:

[If the celebration of eucharist does not follow and the nuptial blessing is omitted, the presider may immediately invite those present to pray the Lord's Prayer. The rite would conclude with the following prayer and a simple blessing taken from the Roman Rite of Marriage. When a nuptial blessing is used the presider may incorporate it into the general intercessions so that they are harmonious but not a duplication. The following concluding prayer would be omitted.]

Presider: Kind and loving God, Creator of the universe, through the saving mystery of Christ, the wedding feast of the Lamb has begun. Hear our prayers for [*Name and Name*]. Strengthen them with your grace and bring to completion the good you have begun in them. Grant this through Christ, our Lord.

Anniversary of Marriage
Option #1

Presider: Since you have come to the table of life to give thanks to God for the gift of married love, let us join our voices in prayer asking that God's gifts of grace may abound in us and in the world.

Petition Leader: Our response today is, **"God, in your goodness, hear us."**

We pray for the gift of a strong faith in God's loving care that [*Name and Name*] may be sustained by it as they continue to live the covenant of marriage. Rejoicing in the Holy Spirit, we ask:

We pray for the gift of generosity that [*Name and Name*] may continue to be instruments of God's loving kindness at home and in society. Rejoicing in the Holy Spirit, we ask:

We pray for the gift of good health and well-being for [*Name and Name*], (for their children,) and for all who are special in their lives. Rejoicing in the Holy Spirit, we ask:

We pray for the gift of wisdom and understanding that the Spirit's grace may continue to guide them in the course of life. Rejoicing in the Holy Spirit, we ask:

We pray for the gift of peace in our world and society that all marriages may flourish free of undue anxieties in daily living. Rejoicing in the Holy Spirit, we ask:

[When the celebration includes Mass the following petition may be added:]
We pray for the gift of unity that the church, nourished on the food and drink of the eucharist, may remain faithful to the gospel of love. Rejoicing in the Holy Spirit, we ask:

We pray for the gift of eternal life for all our beloved dead (especially _____ [*Names of deceased persons significant to the couple*]) that they may enjoy the eternal peace of Christ. Rejoicing in the Holy Spirit, we ask:

Presider: Almighty God, source of all life and goodness, hear our prayers, hasten to help us, and enrich [*Name and Name*] with your grace. We ask this in Jesus' name.

Anniversary of Marriage
Option #2

[These petitions are suitable for a Catholic couple.]

Presider: Let us join our voices in prayer as we call upon God to bring all good things to perfection in Christ.

Petition Leader: Our response is, **"Give us your love and grace, Lord."**

We pray for [*Name and Name*] as they celebrate the years of their married love. May they continue in their resolve to be faithful to the sacrament of marriage. Trusting in God's help, we ask:

We entrust to God's tender care their (children, grandchildren,) relatives and friends. May the divine protection surround them and keep them safe always. Trusting in God's help, we ask:

We look to God to strengthen all marriages, especially those in difficult periods. May the Spirit of Christ sustain spouses and families in the healing love of God. Trusting in God's help, we ask:

We call upon the risen Christ to uphold the church in faith, hope, and love. May all the faithful be blessed with wisdom and understanding on our journey to the kingdom. Trusting in God's help, we ask:

We implore the Holy Spirit to enable world leaders to pursue lasting peace among all nations and peoples. May their efforts bring greater harmony to societies and families. Trusting in God's help, we ask:

We ask God to receive with tender mercy all our beloved dead and those whose hopes were centered on the wedding feast of heaven. May [*Names of deceased persons significant to the couple*] and all the dead rest in peace. Trusting in God's help, we ask:

Presider: Compassionate God, by your loving design you have called [*Name and Name*] to live the mystery of Christ through the sacrament of marriage. In baptism you made them your own. Through grace you sustain them by your Word and the food of the eucharist. Hear our prayers for them and for the world that all may come to the fullness of life in Christ, who lives and reigns with you and the Holy Spirit, one God forever and ever.

Anniversary of Marriage (Twenty-Five Years)

Presider: Let us join together in prayer for [*Name and Name*], giving thanks for twenty-five years of married life and to intercede for an increase of love in our world.

Petition Leader: Our prayer response is, **"Christ, our Life, hear us."**

Called to love one another as Christ loves us, may God enable [*Name and Name*] to continue living the gospel through their commitment to Christ in marriage. With joyful hearts, we pray:

Invited by Christ to follow him in being faithful to God's will, may all the baptized safeguard the life of grace through fidelity to the commandments of the Lord. With joyful hearts, we pray:

Summoned by the Spirit to be instruments of peace and compassion in our world, may we be fortified by God's word as we put our faith into action. With joyful hearts, we pray:

Moved by God's Spirit to be a people of thanksgiving, may [*Name and Name*] continue to sing God's praises in the midst of the church at prayer. With joyful hearts, we pray:

Sustained by the love of Christ, may all the sick experience the tender mercies of God that lead to healing and peace. With joyful hearts, we pray:

Created to be family of unity and peace, may all those who are dear to [*Name and Name*], especially their (children, parents, and) relatives, enjoy the blessings of happiness and mutual care. With joyful hearts, we pray:

Mindful that Christ is the first-born of the dead, may the deceased relatives and friends of [*Name and Name*] be found rejoicing in God's presence. With joyful hearts, we pray:

Presider: Redeeming God, through the resurrection of Christ heaven is wedded to earth and all things find their fullness in the Lord. Hear our prayers and by your grace sustain the church and those called to the sacrament of marriage, particularly [*Name and Name*]. Grant this through Christ, your Beloved and our Savior.

Anniversary of Marriage (Fifty Years)

Presider: Having reaffirmed the marriage vows you exchanged fifty years ago, let us pray that all good things will be sustained by God's grace.

Petition Leader: Our response to each intercession is, **"Spirit of God, be with us."**

By the power of God's love may [*Name and Name*] continue living in mutual and lasting fidelity as husband and wife. Relying on God's care, we pray:

By the light of the gospel may their faith in God and in each other grow stronger with the passing of years. Relying on God's care, we pray:

By the grace of Christ may their experience of God's compassion continue to be a source of spiritual strength, particularly in periods of trial and change. Relying on God's care, we pray:

By the wise counsel of the Spirit may all who are dear to them (especially their children and grandchildren) be guided in paths of holiness and peace. Relying on God's care, we pray:

By the sacramental life of the church may all who belong to Christ be enriched for the works of mercy and justice that serve the needy and poor among us. Relying on God's care, we pray:

By the hope which we have in Christ's resurrection may our hearts be consoled at the death of those we love (especially _____ [the names of persons significant to the couple may be included here]). Relying on God's care, we pray:

Presider: God, ever gracious and kind, look with love upon [*Name and Name*]. You have blessed their marriage and upheld them in your love since the day of their birth. Hear our prayers for them and for the church that confidently trusts you will bring all good things to fulfillment in Christ Jesus, in whose name we pray, now and forever.

Anointing of the Sick
Option #1

[The following may be adapted to a Mass for the Sick with no anointings.]

Presider: In faith we call on God's healing love to uphold us.

[An appropriate response may be sung in place of the following.]

Petition Leader: Our prayer response today is, **"God, hasten to help us."**

Let us pray that all who are seriously ill may be given a courageous faith in God's saving power. Trusting in God's care, we call out:

Let us summon the Spirit to bring consolation to any who are struggling with discouragement and despair in their illness. Trusting in God's care, we call out:

Let us implore the Divine Assistance for all who feel the burden of years or whose minds have begun to fail. Trusting in God's care, we call out:

Let us support with our prayers persons overwhelmed by fear and anxiety in their illness. Trusting in God's care, we call out:

Let us pray to walk in solidarity with all who are in periods of recovery from substance and sexual abuse or struggling to heal from acts of violence. Trusting in God's care, we call out:

Let us pray to bring personal care and companionship to those who feel most alone and alienated by their illness, especially children. Trusting in God's care, we call out:

Let us call down the Divine Wisdom for those who are working to discover cures for deadly diseases and to provide more healthful environments for all people. Trusting in God's care, we call out:

[If there are no anointings, the following petition is omitted and the intercessions conclude with the presider's prayer.]

Let us quietly invoke the Spirit to come as helper and friend to all who are anointed and upon whom we lay our hands in the name of Jesus. [The imposition of hands follows.]

Presider: God of all kindness and compassion, receive the prayers of your church that calls upon your healing love in the name of Jesus, our Redeemer.

Anointing of the Sick
Option #2

[The following may be adapted to a Mass for the Sick with no anointings.]

Presider: As a community of believers in God's saving power, let us call upon the healing love of Christ to be with all the sick and persons in periods of recovery.

Petition Leader: Our prayer response is, **"Compassionate God, hear us."**

We entrust to your care all the sick. May they be given a strong faith in your healing power. Trusting in your love for us, we pray:

We pray for persons facing treatment and care decisions for themselves or those they love. May your wisdom guide them. Trusting in your love for us, we pray:

We ask your blessings upon all health care personnel and caregivers. May they be instruments of your healing and compassion. Trusting in your love for us, we pray:

We rely on your grace to sustain in joyful hope all who are terminally ill. May their love for you help overcome all despair and anxiety. Trusting in your love for us, we pray:

We ask you to renew in body, mind, and spirit any who have been victims of violence or struggling to overcome debilitating addictions. May they find personal prayer a source of strength. Trusting in your love for us, we pray:

We implore your grace to help us provide safe havens for the elderly, to guide medical research, and to assure quality health care for the economically poor among us, especially women and children. Trusting in your love for us, we pray:

We pray that our celebration of Jesus' Paschal mystery and the sacraments of your comforting love will sustain us. May we be fortified in grace throughout life's journey. Trusting in your love for us, we pray:

[If there are no anointings the following petition is omitted and the intercessions conclude with the presider's prayer.]

We call upon your Holy Spirit to move with power over all who are anointed today and upon whom we lay our hands in the Savior's name. [The imposition of hands follows.]

Presider: God, in your mercy turn toward us and hear our prayer. We trust in your saving power to bring us healing, forgiveness, and peace through Christ, our Lord.

Anointing of the Sick (Litany[+])
Option #3

[The following may be adapted to a Mass for the Sick with no anointing.]

Presider: Let us invoke the Spirit as helper and friend in the name of Christ, the Healer.

[The following response may be recited or sung.]

Petition Leader: Our response today is, **"Spirit of mercy, come to our aid!"**

Bless the sick, sustain them in hope, we ask in faith:

Ease their anxieties, free them from pain, we ask in faith:

Forgive their sins, banish any despair, we ask in faith:

Strengthen their faith, deepen their trust, we ask in faith:

Provide for their care, uphold their caregivers, we ask in faith:

Grace their recovery, preserve their lives, we ask in faith:

Embrace the dying, console their families, we ask in faith:

Free your people from all afflictions, keep us united in Christ, we ask in faith:

[If there are no anointings the following petition is omitted and the litany concludes with the presider's prayer.]

Bestow your healing love as we lay our hands on our sisters and brothers in the name of Christ. [The imposition of hands follows.]

Presider: God of mercy, hear our prayers and in your kindness pour forth your healing Spirit to help us. We ask this in the name of Jesus, our Savior.

[+] These petitions are designed to be read as a litany. The proclamation should move quickly but not in a rushed or hurried manner.

Anointing of the Sick

Option #4

[The following may be adapted to a Mass for the Sick with no anointings.]

Presider: The epistle of St. James assures us that the prayer of faith will save those who are sick. Let us raise our voices to intercede on behalf of the sick.

Petition Leader: Our prayer response is, **"O God, show us your mercy and love."**

Bring your healing peace to all who are living with a serious or terminal illness, we pray in faith:

Come with your healing care to families who are emotionally and economically devastated by the illness of a loved one, we pray in faith:

Sustain with your healing compassion those who are abandoned because of the nature of their illness, we pray in faith:

Support with your healing Spirit any whose illness is accompanied by depression and despair, we pray in faith:

Help with your healing power the mentally and physically disabled and any who are struggling to adjust to a permanent injury, we pray in faith:

Enlighten with your wisdom all who are working to discover cures for deadly diseases, we pray in faith:

Bless those who have taken up your mission of compassionate service to the sick, especially caregivers and medical and health-care professionals, we pray in faith:

Bestow forgiveness to the ill who seek your pardon and peace for their sins, we pray in faith:

[If there are no anointings the following petition is omitted and the intercessions conclude with the presider's prayer.]

Bring life and renewed health to our sisters and brothers upon whom we lay our hands in the name of Jesus. [The imposition of hands follows.]

Presider: Gracious God, hear us as we call upon your healing love in solidarity with our sisters and brothers who are ill. Uphold them in your mercy through Christ, our Redeemer.

Anointing of the Sick (For HIV-Positive Persons)

[The following intercessions may be adapted to other life-threatening illnesses as pastoral circumstances require; they may also be adapted to a Mass for the Sick with no anointings.]

Presider: Let us pray that God's love for all persons will be a source of strength, hope, healing, and peace.

Petition Leader: Our response to each petition will be a moment of silent prayer. [Petition leader, please allow for a sufficient pause after each petition.]

For any who are living with AIDS or AIDS-related illness. May they be fortified by personal prayer and strong faith.

For persons who are dying from AIDS, especially infants and children. May God's tender compassion lead them gently into the new creation.

For caregivers and all who serve HIV-positive persons through health-care professions. May each person be an instrument of God's healing presence.

For medical research as it works to find effective immunizations against AIDS and related illnesses. May God's Spirit bless their efforts.

For government leaders and representatives upon whose vote federal funding for AIDS research and health care benefits depends. May public officials act in the spirit of justice and care.

For faith communities, especially those that bear the name of Christ. May our houses of prayer be rich havens of compassion and friendship.

[If there are no anointings the following petition is omitted and the intercessions conclude with the presider's prayer.]

For all who seek God's comforting love in this sacrament of healing, forgiveness, and peace. May those upon whom we lay our hands know the blessing of Christ in the Spirit. [The imposition of hands follows.]

Presider: God, abounding in kindness and compassion, hear our prayers especially those within the quiet of our hearts. Show us your mercy and love through Christ, the Healer.

Viaticum

[A number of petitions are included here. The presider or minister may select three or four that are appropriate to the circumstances.]

Presider: United in faith and hope, let us pray to the one Savior of all peoples, Jesus Christ.

Petition Leader:

You came that we may have fullness of life; we trust in your word: Lord, have mercy on our brother/sister.
Assembly: Lord, have mercy.

You gave your life in ransom for the many; we remember your love. Christ, have mercy on our brother/sister.
Assembly: Christ, have mercy.

You promised to be refreshment for our souls; we rely on your mercy. Lord, have mercy on our brother/sister.
Assembly: Lord, have mercy.

You came among us in the Spirit's power; we long for the oil of gladness. Christ, have mercy on our brother/sister.
Assembly: Christ, have mercy.

You revealed yourself to be the Bread of Life; we set our hearts on the feast of heaven. Lord, have mercy on our brother/sister.
Assembly: Lord, have mercy.

You are the new covenant of peace; we believe you alone are the Holy One who takes away our sins. Christ have mercy on our brother/sister.
Assembly: Christ, have mercy.

You are the Light that dispels the darkness of sadness and death; we are the people who long to see your face. Lord have mercy on our brother/sister.
Assembly: Lord, have mercy.

[If the liturgy of the eucharist is not celebrated the litany concludes with the Lord's Prayer followed by communion as Viaticum.]

Funeral, Wake, or Memorial Service (Advent)

Presider: In hope we await the coming of Christ who will raise up our mortal bodies and fashion them like his own in glory. Let us pray in a spirit of faith, hope, and love, particularly for [*Name*].

Petition Leader: Our prayer response is, **"Come, Lord Jesus, set us free."**

In baptism, [*Name*] was given the hope of seeing your salvation. Release him/her from death and let him/her see your kindness, we pray:

You came to set prisoners free. Come, Key of David and open the gates of God's kingdom for our brother/sister, we pray:

Mary trusted that God's word would be fulfilled. Come, Word of Peace, and in your loving kindness welcome [*Name*] into the company of heaven, we pray:

You are the compassion of God. Come with mercy and consolation for [*Name's*] family (especially _____ [the names of close relatives may be included here]), we pray:

John the Baptist prepared your way. Come, wisdom of our God, and prepare us to meet you when our earthly pilgrimage has ended, we pray: You are the Radiant Dawn of eternal light. Come, Sun of Justice, and shine on all who have died in your peace, we pray:

You are our Resurrection and Life. Come and raise up the creation you redeemed through the blood of your cross, we pray:

Presider: Jesus, our Emmanuel, save us we pray. Receive the soul of your servant for, indeed, you are our lasting peace who lives and reigns forever and ever.

Funeral, Wake, or Memorial Service (Christmas Season)

Presider: In the birth of Jesus the day of salvation has dawned for us. We pray that the Word-Made-Flesh will bestow on our brother/sister the fullness of risen life.

Petition Leader: Our response is, **"Christ, our Light, hear our prayer."**

In baptism, [*Name*] was given the hope of sharing everlasting life. Now that the kindness and love of God our Savior have appeared, may he/she be received with tender mercy. We pray:

In sending us Jesus Christ, God has not forsaken us. May the Spirit of consolation be with [*Name's*] family (especially _____). We pray:

Jesus came to bring glad tidings to the lowly and the broken-hearted. May all the dead see the saving power of God restoring their life in the reign of heaven. We pray:

Born of Mary, as one like ourselves, Jesus accepted death on the cross to cleanse us of sin. Through the eucharist may our brother/sister be cleansed of any sin by the perfect sacrifice of Christ. We pray:

Christ came among us filled with enduring love. May the Spirit of Christ fill us with an enduring love for God that we may be united with Christ our Light when our earthly journey has ended. We pray:

Presider: Saving God, you sent your beloved Son into the world to be its true light. Our brother/sister walked by the light of faith. Hear our prayers that your servant will see your glory, through Christ our Peace.

Funeral, Wake, or Memorial Service (Lent)

Presider: Our brother's/sister's journey in faith has ended. Let us pray that God will receive him/her and all the dead with tender mercy.

Petition Leader: Our response is, **"Show us your mercy and love, O God!"**

Jesus accepted death on the cross out of love for the sinner. May [*Name*], who was signed with the cross of Christ in baptism, find kindly welcome in the reign of God. We ask in faith:

Jesus left the eucharist to the church as a memorial of his passion. May [*Name's*] communion in the body and blood of Christ find fulfillment in the banquet of heaven. We ask in faith:

Jesus prepared his disciples for his impending death. May the gospel of life prepare us to live reverently and justly that we may arrive at the resurrection when our life's pilgrimage has ended. We ask in faith:

Jesus met the woman at the well and invited her to faith. May we come to know Christ on our life's journey and be filled with a faith to sustain us in time of trial. We ask in faith:

Jesus shared Martha and Mary's grief at the death of their brother, Lazarus. May God's consoling Spirit be with [*Name's*] family to uphold them. We ask in faith:

Jesus called Lazarus to come forth from his tomb. May all our beloved dead rise at the Word of God to the glory of the resurrection on the last day. We ask in faith:

Presider: God of compassion, your sent Christ into the world so that all who believe might have eternal life. Hear our prayers and strengthen our hope that in the dying and rising of Jesus salvation has been won for all. We ask this through Christ, your suffering Servant and our risen Savior.

Funeral, Wake, or Memorial Service (Easter Season)

Presider: Jesus Christ, risen from the dead, has bequeathed to us the promise of a new heaven and a new earth. With Easter hope let us pray for the living and the dead.

Petition Leader: Our response is, **"Risen Savior, have mercy on us."**

In baptism, [*Name*] was called to die with Christ so as to live a new life in the Lord. Now that his/her pilgrimage on earth has ended may he/she share a like resurrection. We pray:

At dawn on the first day of the week the women received the news of Christ's resurrection. May our brother/sister receive from Christ the good news of risen life as eternity dawns for him/her. We pray:

The wedding feast of the Lamb has begun. May our brother/sister who shared with us the bread of life and the cup of blessing be seated at the heavenly banquet. We pray:

Christ has been set apart by God to be the judge of the living and the dead. May we be found clothed in justice, peace, compassion, and love when we are called from this life. We pray:

God has given us a new birth which draws its life from the resurrection of Jesus. May all our beloved dead be born into eternal life through the kindness of God. We pray:

The Risen Christ proclaimed peace to his disciples. May the Holy Spirit of peace and consolation sustain [*Name's*] family. We pray:

Thomas doubted the news of the resurrection. May any who are overshadowed by doubt and heartbreak at the death of a loved one experience the healing love of Christ. We pray:

Presider: Christ Jesus, Son of the living God, you have conquered sin and death. Hear our prayers for your servant [*Name*] and quicken our faith in your resurrection, for you live and reign forever and ever.

Funeral, Wake, or Memorial Service (Ordinary Time)
Option #1

Presider: Let us draw consolation through prayer calling upon Christ, our Resurrection and Life.

Petition Leader: As we pray today let us join our voices in asking: **"Christ, our Life, hear our prayer."**

In baptism [*Name*] was joined to Christ and given the Holy Spirit as first gift. May the Spirit now bring him/her to the fullness of risen life in Christ, we pray:

Jesus bore our humanity even to death on a cross. May the cross of Christ and the power of the Savior's resurrection bring strength to [*Name's*] family, (especially _____ [the names of family members may be included here]), we pray:

In Christ we are shown the compassionate face of God. May God's mercy be with us and particularly any who are suffering in body, mind, or spirit, we pray:

In hope we await a new heaven and a new earth where every tear will be wiped away. May _____ [any pre-deceased family members may be included here], who have preceded [*Name*] in death, be counted among the blessed, we pray:

We are summoned to bear each other's burdens. May the Spirit of God strengthen all who serve the sick and dying, particularly hospice personnel and volunteers, doctors, nurses, home health aids, and social service workers, we pray:

We believe that hope will not leave us disappointed. Confidently let us entrust to God those persons whose faith and hope is challenged by sickness and death and also any personal needs that call out for God's healing and peace. [Petition leader, allow for a sufficient pause for quiet prayer.] We pray:

Presider: Merciful God, you are the beginning and end of all life. Hear our prayers, console our hearts, and strengthen us in the hope of resurrection. We ask this through Christ Jesus, our Resurrection and Life.

Funeral, Wake, or Memorial Service (Ordinary Time)
Option #2

Presider: Let us pray.

Petition Leader: Because we believe that our prayers are graciously received by God, together let us ask in faith, **"God of mercy, hear our prayer."**

For [*Name*] who was given the promise of eternal life in baptism. May Christ bid him/her a kindly welcome and grant him/her perfect peace. We ask in faith:

For [*Name's*] family (especially _____ [the names of relatives may be included here]), may the promise of Jesus to raise up all humanity and heal its wounds be for them a source of comfort and healing. We ask in faith:

For all who find life burdensome and struggle to cope with pain, uncertainty, and heartbreak. May the Spirit of God strengthen the weary with renewed hope and a courageous faith. We ask in faith:

For the dead who do not yet see the glory of God. May Christ, the compassionate Savior, banish the darkness of death and bring all the dead into the reign of eternal light. We ask in faith:

For our world, wherever it is longing for a true and enduring peace that the Spirit of truth will plant the seeds of the gospel of peace into every human heart. We ask in faith:

[The following petition may be omitted when Mass is not celebrated.]
For ourselves as we gather as the body of Christ around the eucharistic table. May the food of the eucharist draw us closer to one another and to the presence of Christ, who promises to raise us on the last day. We ask in faith:

For any particular needs and concerns, let us now pray quietly. [Petition leader, please allow for a sufficient pause.] We ask in faith:

Presider: Redeeming God, you called [*Name*] to walk as a child of the light in baptism. Hear our prayers on his/her behalf which we raise to you in the name of Jesus Christ, the Light of Life.

Funeral, Wake, or Memorial Service
(Youth or Young Adult)

Presider: Let us pray mindful of families who grieve the loss of a young person.

Petition Leader: Our response today is, **"Consoling Spirit, be with us."**

[*Name*] was signed with the oil of gladness at baptism. May the Spirit, who raised Jesus from the dead, bring him/her into the reign of heaven. Trusting in God's love, we pray:

Jesus came to remove our robe of mourning. May the compassionate Savior place on [*Name*] the mantle of everlasting joy. Trusting in God's love, we pray:

[The following petition may be omitted for pastoral reasons or circumstances.]
[*Name*] celebrated God's love in our midst at the table of the Lord. May Christ receive him/her into the banquet of life in heaven. Trusting in God's love, we pray:

Many young people die in the noontime of life. May those who die at an early age be received with mercy and love in the land of the living. Trusting in God's love, we pray:

Every life is precious in God's sight. May [*Name's*] family find hope knowing that God is abounding in kindness and compassion. Trusting in God's love, we pray:

Every death leaves a void in our lives. May [*Name's*] friends and classmates draw strength and courage from their faith and families. Trusting in God's love, we pray:

For all of us gathered here in prayer. May God's Word be our light in a time of darkness (and the eucharist sustain us in hope). Trusting in God's love, we pray:

Presider: God in heaven, we believe that your love leads us to restful waters and a place of everlasting peace. May Jesus Christ, the eternal Shepherd of your people, give [*Name*] kindly welcome in the land of the living. We ask this through Christ our Lord.

Funeral, Wake, or Memorial Service
(Tragic or Violent Death)

Presider: Let us pray trusting in God's consoling love.

Petition Leader: Our response will be a moment of silent prayer after each petition. [Petition leader, please allow for a sufficient pause after each intercession.]

Mindful that Jesus loved us even to his death, let us entrust [*Name*] to the compassionate Christ who promised to raise us on the last day.

Remembering that in baptism [*Name*] was signed with the cross of Christ and has shared in the passion of the Lord, let us pray that he/she may share in Christ's victory over death.

Believing that God does not abandon us in our sorrow, let us implore God's consoling Spirit to uphold [*Name's*] family in this time of grief.

Knowing how violence and tragedy disrupt the harmony and peace of families and communities, let us ask for the grace of God's healing love to be with us.

Trusting that a new heaven and new earth await us, let us prayerfully remember all whose lives are marked by heartbreak and who long for the reign of God.

Recognizing that violence and cruelty have no part in God's plan, let us invoke Christ to pour out the Holy Spirit of peace and respect into every human heart.

[If Mass is to be celebrated the following petition may be included.]
Grateful for [*Name's*] life and faith in Christ, the Bread of Life, let us pray that our participation in Christ's sacrifice will sustain us as we continue life's journey.

Presider: Redeeming God, hear our prayers and those in the silence of our hearts. Be ever close to [*Name's*] family and friends and by the power of your Word and Spirit uphold us in your love. Grant this in Jesus' name.

Funeral, Wake, or Memorial Service
(For a Baptized Child)

[These intercessions are suitable for a liturgy or prayer service in which age-mates of the deceased child participate.]

Presider: Jesus told us that in heaven there is no more crying and sadness, only happiness with God. Let us pray that [*Name*] now shares in this joy.

Petition Leader: Our response is, **"Jesus, hear our prayer."**

When [*Name*] was baptized he/she became a child of God. May he/she share the joy of all God's children in the new home of heaven. We pray:

[*Name*] was given the light of Christ. May he/she live in the light of God's love forever. We pray:

Jesus came to take away all pain and hurt. May God's help be with [*Name's*] family and friends. We pray:

Jesus taught us not to be afraid for God loves us always. May God's Holy Spirit take away our fears and give us peace. We pray:

[If the deceased child had received the eucharist the following petition may be included.]

[*Name*] shared with us the bread of life. May Jesus welcome him/her to God's table in heaven to share the joy of the angels and saints. We pray:

Presider: God, today our hearts are sad because we have to say good-bye to someone we love. We know one day you will turn our sorrow into joy, so we ask you to help us believe that [*Name*] is safe with you and Jesus forever.

Funeral, Wake, or Memorial Service
(For an Unbaptized Child)

[This may also be used for an unbaptized child who died at birth. It contains an optional petition for the mother if she should be seriously ill.]

Presider: Let us call upon Christ to comfort [*Name(s) of parents/parent*] at this sad time and with all who mourn the loss of a child.

Petition Leader: Our response is, **"Christ, our Life, uphold us."**

Jesus, you are the compassion of God. May your promise to raise us on the last day console [*Name(s) of parents/parent*]. Trusting in your love for us, we pray:

Jesus, you promised to prepare a place for us in the kingdom of God. May your love embrace [*Name of child or this child*] with new life in heaven. Trusting in your love for us, we pray:

Jesus, you bring us to birth through your life-giving Spirit. May your Holy Spirit strengthen the faith of [*Name(s) of parents/parent*] in their/her/his sorrow. Trusting in your love for us, we pray:

Jesus, you died and rose that all may come to life in God's reign. May all who mourn the loss of a child be sustained by the hope of resurrection. Trusting in your love for us, we pray:

[The following petition may be included if the mother is seriously ill.]
Jesus, born of Mary, you are our lasting peace. May your Spirit and the prayers of your Mother bring healing and peace to [*Name of mother*]. Trusting in your love for us, we pray:

[The Lord's Prayer may follow, and the prayer of the faithful concludes with the presider's prayer.]

Presider: With hearts that long for God's kingdom, let us pray in the words Jesus gave us: Our Father . . .

Loving God, you are the Source of our life and our Eternal Home. Hear our prayers for [*Name(s) of parents/parent*]. Carry them/her/him gently through this time of sorrow. We entrust to you the life of their/her/his child. May your love reunite us in the peace of heaven through Jesus Christ, your Son, who lives and reigns with you and the Holy Spirit, one God, forever and ever.

Funeral, Wake, or Memorial Service (For a Stillborn)

Presider: Let us call upon Christ to comfort [*Name(s) of parents/parent*] at this sad time and all who mourn the loss of a child.

Petition Leader: Our response is, **"Christ, our Life, uphold us."**

Jesus, you are the compassion of God. May your promise to raise us on the last day console [*Name(s) of parents/parent*]. Trusting in your love for us, we pray:

Jesus, you promised to prepare a place for us in the kingdom of God. May [*Name of child or this child*], whose eyes did not see the light of this world, behold your face in heaven. Trusting in your love for us, we pray:

Jesus, you died and rose that all may come to life in God's reign. May all who mourn the loss of a child be sustained by the hope of resurrection. Trusting in your love for us, we pray:

Jesus, born of Mary, you are our lasting peace. May your Spirit and the prayers of your Mother bring us healing and peace in time of sorrow. Trusting in your love for us, we pray:

[The Lord's Prayer may follow, and the prayer of the faithful concludes with the presider's prayer.]

Presider: With hearts that long for God's kingdom, let us pray in the words Jesus gave us: Our Father . . .

Loving God, you are the Source of our life and our Eternal Home. Hear our prayers for [*Name(s) of parents/parent*]. Carry them/her/him gently through this time of sorrow. Bring us all to birth in the peace of heaven through Jesus Christ, your Son, who lives and reigns with you and the Holy Spirit, one God, forever and ever.

Funeral, Wake, or Memorial Service
(For a Deceased Mother and Child)

[These petitions may be used when a mother and infant have both died in childbirth. It should be adapted to the pastoral and liturgical circumstances.]

Presider: Let us call upon God's consoling love to be with us in this time of sorrow.

Petition Leader: Our response is, "Lord, have mercy."

We entrust to your loving care [*Names of deceased mother and child*]. May they be united in the peace of heaven where there is no sorrow or pain. Relying on your love to sustain us, we pray:

[If both mother and child were baptized.]

We ask you to fulfill for [*Names of deceased mother and child*] the promises they were given in baptism. May your love bring them to new birth in the land of the living. Relying on your love to sustain us, we pray:

[If only the mother was baptized.]

We ask you to fulfill for [*Name of deceased mother*] the promise given to her in baptism. May the life and faith she longed to share with her child be brought to fulfillment in your presence. Relying on your love to sustain us, we pray:

We believe your love raises us to new life. May [*Name of child or this child*] behold your face in company with the angels and saints. Relying on your love to sustain us, we pray:

We call upon your consoling Spirit to uphold [*Name of deceased woman's*] family, (especially _____ [Names of family members may be included]). May their faith be strengthened in this moment of sorrow. Relying on your love to sustain us, we pray:

We long for your healing love to guide us gently through times of doubt and grief. May the cross of Christ, which we share, fill us with hope and peace of heart. Relying on your love to sustain us, we pray:

We look to the day when Christ will come to gather your faithful people into the new creation. May we continue our journey in faith with our hearts set upon the joy of eternal life. Relying on your love to sustain us, we pray:

[If the liturgy of the eucharist is not celebrated at this time, the Lord's Prayer follows with the customary introduction. Otherwise, the intercessions are brought to a close with the following prayer.]

Presider: God of our life, receive our prayers. In your mercy, pour out your consoling Spirit that we may be sustained in faith and hope. Grant this through Jesus Christ, our Hope of Resurrection.

Funeral, Wake, or Memorial Service (For a Priest)

Presider: As a priest, [*Name*] interceded for the needs of God's people at the table of the Lord. Now let us intercede on his behalf and for all the dead.

Petition Leader: Our prayer response is, **"God, in your mercy, hear us."**

In baptism, [*Name*] was joined to God's priestly people and anointed with the oil of gladness. May Christ, the eternal Priest, receive this servant into the heavenly sanctuary. We pray:

[*Name*] responded in faith to Christ's call in the Spirit to a life of priestly service. May Christ bestow on him the crown of life now that his earthly pilgrimage has ended. We pray:

[*Name*] proclaimed the tender mercy of God in word and sacrament. May our compassionate God embrace him with love and mercy. We pray:

[For a religious priest.]
[*Name*] consecrated his life to Christ as [*Name of religious community*]. May the Holy Spirit consecrate him in the joy of Christ eternally. We pray:

[For the relatives, religious community, or parish of the deceased priest.]
As God's people we long for the New Jerusalem. May [*Names of relatives, community, or parish*] be consoled by the gospel's promise of a new creation where death is destroyed forever. We pray:

Trusting in God's power to raise all people to the fullness of life, may all the dead rejoice in the resurrection of the just. We pray:

Gathered together to celebrate our life in Christ, may the word of God and the eucharist strengthen our hope of sharing in the heavenly banquet. We pray:

Presider: Gracious God, hear the prayers of your priestly people who invoke your mercy and love for [*Name of deceased priest*]. Uphold us by your Spirit and bring us to the splendor of your reign where Jesus is Lord forever and ever.

Funeral, Wake, or Memorial Service (For a Deacon)

Presider: As a deacon, [*Name*] served the needs of God's people. Let us pray on his behalf in the name of Christ, our Life.

Petition Leader: Our prayer response is, **"Christ, our Life, hear us."**

In baptism, [*Name*] was joined to Christ in the household of the church. May Christ welcome him into the community of heaven. We pray:

[*Name*] responded in faith to Christ's call in the Spirit to be of service to the church. May Christ give him rest from his labor. We pray:

[*Name*] proclaimed the gospel of God's tender mercy. May our compassionate God embrace him with love and mercy. We pray:

[For a religious deacon.]
[*Name*] consecrated his life to Christ as [*Name of religious community*]. May the Holy Spirit consecrate him in the joy of Christ eternally. We pray:

[For a married or widowed permanent deacon.]
As God's people we long for the New Jerusalem. May [*Names of family members*] be consoled by the gospel's promise of a new creation where death is destroyed forever. We pray:

Trusting in God's power to raise all people to the fullness of life, may all the dead rejoice in the resurrection of the just. We pray:

Gathered together to celebrate our life in Christ, may the word of God and the eucharist strengthen our hope of sharing in the heavenly banquet. We pray:

Presider: Gracious God, hear the prayers of your church that invokes your mercy and love for [*Name of deceased deacon*]. Uphold us by your Spirit and bring us to the splendor of your reign where Jesus is Lord forever and ever.

Funeral, Wake, or Memorial Service (For a Religious)

Presider: Mindful that God's love is everlasting, let us entrust our brother/sister, [*Name*], to Christ, now that his/her earthly journey has ended.

Petition Leader: Our prayer response is, **"Christ, graciously hear us."**

In baptism, [*Name*] was joined to Christ and sealed with the Holy Spirit. May he/she rejoice in the fullness of life that the Spirit bestows. We pray:

[*Name*] responded in faith to Christ's call in the Spirit to live as a member of [*Name of religious community*] for the sake of God's reign. May the Spirit of Christ bring his/her consecration to fulfillment in God's presence. We pray:

[*Name*] celebrated the gospel of God's tender mercy at the eucharistic table. May our compassionate God welcome him/her into the banquet of life. We pray:

[*Name*] shared his/her gifts generously as _____ [a ministry or apostolate may be mentioned here]. May he/she rest from his/her labors and his/her good deeds be pleasing in God's sight. We pray:

We are a people who long to see God's face. May all the dead rejoice in the presence of the living God in company with Mary, [*Name of a special saint or community founder*], and all the saints. We pray:

We rely on God's love to sustain us through every season of life. May [*Names of family members and religious community*] draw consolation and hope from the gospel's promise of risen life. We pray:

We remember that we are God's servants in life and death. May the word of God and the eucharist strengthen us to live as God's holy people. We pray:

Presider: Gracious God, hear the prayers of your church that invokes your mercy and love for [*Name of deceased religious*]. Through the power of your Spirit sustain us in faith and hope, and bring us to the joy of Christ's resurrection, who lives and reigns forever and ever.

Committal Service

Presider: As we return [*Name's*] body/ashes to the earth, let us pray in joyful hope.

Petition Leader: Our response is, **"Clothe him/her with the robe of salvation!"**

You raised the dead to life; may our brother/sister find kindly welcome in the land of the living. We pray to the Lord:

In baptism [*Name*] was given the hope of entering the new creation; may he/she rejoice in the company of the saints. We pray to the Lord:

[*Name*] proclaimed the death and resurrection of Jesus at the table of the eucharist; may God grant him/her a place at the heavenly banquet. We pray to the Lord:

[If the deceased person was married and it is pastorally sensitive the following may be added.]
[*Name*] was faithful to the covenant of marriage; may God fulfill for him/her the covenant of redemption sealed by the blood of Christ. We pray to the Lord:

[For a deceased priest or deacon.]
[*Name*] was called to share in the ministry of Jesus Christ; may Christ bestow on him the joy promised to the Lord's faithful servants. We pray to the Lord:

[For a deceased religious.]
[*Name*] consecrated his/her life to Christ for the sake of God's reign; may God receive this servant into the New Jerusalem. We pray to the Lord:

[For a person who died after a long illness.]
God called [*Name*] to share in the passion of Jesus through (mental and) physical weakness; may the power of God's Spirit raise him/her to new life. We pray to the Lord:

We believe God's love makes all things new; may [*Name*] who shared this hope be given eternal rest. We pray to the Lord:

[The Lord's Prayer follows.]

Feasts and Memorials of Mary and the Saints

St. Elizabeth Seton (January 4)

Presider: Let us pray that our lives will reflect the light of God's love as did the life of St. Elizabeth Seton.

Petition Leader: Our response today is, **"Christ, our Light, hear our prayer."**

The love of God has appeared among us offering salvation to all people. May the church constantly surrender itself to the mission entrusted to it by the Lord of Light. With joyful hearts, we pray:

The love of Christ impels the hearts of believers to live no longer for themselves but for Christ. May the Spirit strengthen us to live unselfishly for the sake of the gospel. With joyful hearts, we pray:

The light of God's love has shone in our hearts that we may make the glory of Christ known. May all who are dedicated to ministries of teaching and service be fortified by the intercession of St. Elizabeth Seton. With joyful hearts, we pray:

The compassion of God is our strength in time of trial. May widows with children be encouraged by Elizabeth Seton's trust and experience her prayerful help. With joyful hearts, we pray:

[The following may be added where appropriate.]
The Spirit of love consecrates us to be a new creation in Christ. May the Spirit, who inspired Mother Seton to be of service to the church, bless the lives and ministries of the Sisters of Charity she established. With joyful hearts, we pray:

Presider: God in heaven, we praise the wonders of your love revealed in the incarnation of your eternal Word. Hear our prayers, and by your grace may we, like Elizabeth Seton, continue to give vitality to the gospel. Grant this in Jesus' name.

St. John Neumann (January 5)

Presider: Drawn to Christ by the light of faith, St. John Neumann served the Most Holy Redeemer unselfishly. Let us pray that Christ will continue to raise up a servant church abounding in faith and charity.

Petition Leader: Our response today is, **"Christ, our Redeemer, hear us."**

For the church as it celebrates the birth of the Savior; may its proclamation of the gospel continue to draw all peoples to Christ. As we rejoice in the birth of Jesus, we pray:

For the Catholic bishops of America; may they be filled with the Spirit's wisdom and inspired by St. John Neumann's zeal for the spiritual welfare of God's people. As we rejoice in the birth of Jesus, we pray:

For all who minister to youth through Catholic education; may educators be blessed with gifts that lead others to Christ. As we rejoice in the birth of Jesus, we pray:

For immigrants in our land; may the pastoral and sacramental ministry of the church be a source of strength for all who are building a new life in the United States. As we rejoice in the birth of Jesus, we pray:

For a deepening of faith in the eucharistic presence of Christ; may the Spirit guide all Christians to know the risen Savior in the breaking of bread. As we rejoice in the birth of Jesus, we pray:

For all who serve God under adverse conditions; may the prayers of St. John Neumann and his example of selfless dedication be a source of encouragement. As we rejoice in the birth of Jesus, we pray:

Presider: Loving God, in Christ you have given us plenteous redemption. Receive our prayers and the intercession of your servant, St. John Neumann, who gave himself totally to Christ, who lives and reigns forever.

Blessed André Bessette (January 6)

May the prayers of Blessed André Bessette help us to be a living edifice for Christ in the Spirit. We pray:

[Also see "Any Saint or Blessed," pages 170-171.]

St. Marguerite Bourgeoys (January 12, Canada)

Presider: Grateful for God's gifts of grace that abound in the church, let us pray to be joyful in our service to God and neighbor as was St. Marguerite Bourgeoys.

Petition Leader: Our response today is, **"Loving God, hear us."**

You blessed Marguerite with a courageous faith that enabled her to endure hardship for the sake of the gospel. May our faith grow stronger that we may be reliable servants of your Word. We pray to the Lord:

You sustained Marguerite in the wilderness of Montreal with your Holy Spirit. May your Spirit uphold all who serve your people under adverse conditions. We pray to the Lord:

You gave Marguerite a generous heart that remained open to the poor, especially children. May our hearts be open to the needs of others in our own time. We pray to the Lord:

Your servant rejoiced in the food of the eucharist. May your church be always grateful for the gift of Christ's sacramental presence. We pray to the Lord:

You sent Marguerite as a light to the native peoples and settlers of Canada. May missionaries who leave the security of their homeland be carriers of the light of universal peace. We pray to the Lord:

[The following may be added where appropriate.]
You placed Marguerite under the special patronage of the Mother of God. May the sisters of the Congregation of Notre Dame, which she founded, continue to know Mary's help in all their endeavors. We pray to the Lord:

Presider: Gracious God, how wonderfully you fill the hungry with good things! Hear our prayer and receive our praise as we remember your servant, Marguerite. Like her may we find lasting joy in your presence, through Christ, our Lord.

St. Francis de Sales (January 24)

Presider: Let us invoke the Spirit of Christ that all the baptized may grow in holiness.

Petition Leader: Our response today is, **"Spirit of truth, fill us."**

Through the proclamation of the gospel may the hearts of all believers be filled with reverence for God and God's creation. We pray:

Through the teaching of the church may all Christians aspire to holiness of life and union with Christ. We pray:

Through the prayers of St. Francis de Sales may all who labor to build up the church community, especially the Catholic press and publishing companies, be animated by the Spirit of unity. We pray:

Through our celebration of the eucharist, may we know the forgiveness of God in our lives and be more forgiving of others who offend us. We pray:

[The following petition may be added where appropriate.]
Through the grace of the Holy Spirit, may the Visitation nuns, co-founded by St. Francis de Sales, be sustained in their consecration to Christ. We pray:

Through the love Christ has for the church, may all the faithful departed rejoice in the company of saints forever. We pray:

Presider: God in heaven, receive our prayers on this memorial of St. Francis de Sales. As he labored to restore unity and peace to your church, so may our efforts to promote unity among Christians be guided by the Spirit of Christ, your Son. Grant this in Jesus' name.

Conversion of St. Paul (January 25)

Presider: Let us pray that the gift of faith will flourish in every human heart.

Petition Leader: Our response today is a moment of silent prayer to the Holy Spirit after each petition. [Petition leader, please allow for a sufficient pause after each petition.]

For Pope [*Name*] and the church's bishops. May their teaching ministry be guided by the Holy Spirit and the prayers of St. Paul.

For missionaries who herald the gospel throughout the world. May their efforts to spread the good news be fruitful in the Lord.

For persons who are actively hostile toward Christianity. May the Holy Spirit bring about a change of heart in the church's enemies.

For those whose newfound faith in Christ alienates them from family and friends. May the love of Christ enable them to endure all things.

For the work of Catholic communications. May all who promote Christ and the church through publications and broadcasting be instruments of unity and peace.

For all who died hoping to know the power of Christ's resurrection (especially _____). May they rejoice with St. Paul in God's presence.

Presider: Loving God, we all stand in need of your grace. Deepen our faith in the gospel that our lives may lead others to Christ. Send the light of faith to those who do not know your saving Word. We ask this in Jesus' name.

St. Thomas Aquinas (January 28)

Presider: Nourished on the bread of God's Word, let us pray that, like St. Thomas Aquinas, all may grow in their knowledge and love for God.

Petition Leader: Our response today is, **"Jesus, Word of Life, hear us."**

For the church as it opens the scriptures and nourishes the faithful of Christ with the good news; may all bishops, homilists, theologians, and Bible scholars be united in their ministries and ideals. We ask in faith:

For the people of God who seek to feast at Wisdom's table; may the Spirit lead sincere believers to the fullness of truth in Christ. We ask in faith:

For pastoral musicians and composers of sacred music; may their works serve to deepen in the church at prayer the wonder of the divine presence. We ask in faith:

For Catholic universities and houses of study under the patronage of St. Thomas Aquinas; may these places of learning nurture students to be strong in their love for God and neighbor. We ask in faith:

For spiritual directors and confessors; may this ministry continue to serve all who thirst for greater intimacy with God. We ask in faith:

Presider: God in heaven, hear our prayers and sustain us in the Spirit of truth who endowed St. Thomas Aquinas with rich gifts of the mind and soul. By the Spirit's power may we all come to full maturity in Christ, the Word of Life, who lives and reigns with you and the Holy Spirit, one God forever and ever.

St. John Bosco (January 31)

Presider: Let us pray, especially remembering young people in need of spiritual guides.

Petition Leader: Our prayer response today is, **"Jesus, joy of the saints, hear us."**

For youths who have been left spiritually orphaned in our world; may they come to know the church as a reliable haven of compassion and truth. We pray:

For any who are gifted with prophecy as was St. John Bosco; may the Spirit's gifts be used for the good of others. We pray:

For the gift of humor and joy; may our love for God readily show itself in our zeal for life. We pray:

For all who work to abolish exploitation of children in overseas factories; may people of goodwill never tire in freeing children from unjust labor practices. We pray:

For all who work with delinquent youths, particularly in detention centers; may this ministry flourish through the grace of the Holy Sprit. We pray:

For persons who earn their livelihood in the circus arts; may they follow the example of Don Bosco and use their talents to draw others to Christ. We pray:

[The following may be added where appropriate.]
For the Salesian community founded by Don Bosco; may the holiness of their lives provide convincing witness of God's love, especially for youth. We pray:

Presider: God, you lovingly showered St. John Bosco with special gifts which he used in service to youth. Hear our prayers, and may the spiritual blessings you send us be used generously, especially for the moral welfare of young people. Grant this in the name of Jesus.

St. Blase (Blessing of Throats, February 3)

May the healing love of God bring renewed health to all the sick, and may the divine protection be with all who seek blessing today through the prayers of St. Blase. We pray:

[Also see "Any Saint or Blessed," pages 170-171.]

St. Paul Miki and Companions (February 6)

Presider: Let us pray that the faith of Christians will remain strong throughout life.

Petition Leader: Our prayer response is, **"Christ, uphold us, we pray."**

For the Catholic church throughout the world, may its rich diversity be rooted in the one life-giving faith in Jesus Christ. We call out in faith:

For the Catholic community in Japan, may the death of St. Paul Miki and the martyrs of Nagasaki continue to be a source of inspiration to believers. We call out in faith:

For all who suffer hardship and torture because of their faith in Christ, may they never cease to draw life from the cross of the Redeemer. We call out in faith:

For all who labor to promote harmony and respect among races and cultures, may all prejudices give way to the Spirit's work of unity and peace. We call out in faith:

For persons who abandon faith in Christ in time of personal or cultural upheaval, may the Holy Spirit renew the grace of their baptism into the body of Christ. We call out in faith:

Presider: Christ Jesus, by your cross you have brought new life to the world. Through the cross of martyrdom you gave Paul Miki and companions a share in your suffering and, indeed, your glory. May we find strength in their witness and be strong in our faith. We pray in your name, Lord, for you live and reign forever.

St. Scholastica (February 10)

Presider: Let our prayers seek God's grace that all may come to new life in Christ.

Petition Leader: Our prayer response is, **"God of blessing, hear us."**

Christ Jesus, you proclaimed as blessed those who hear God's word and keep it. May our contemplation of your gospel deepen our unity with the Trinity. In your name we ask:

Christ Jesus, you raised up St. Scholastica as the mother of western monasticism. May women who are consecrated to you as contemplative religious be strengthened by her prayers. In your name we ask:

Christ Jesus, in you Wisdom has prepared her table. May all who come to feast on your word and sacraments be filled with every grace and blessing. In your name we ask:

Christ Jesus, you taught that the gifts we freely receive we should give as gift. May we be filled with a generous love for others as befits your disciples. In your name we ask:

Christ Jesus, you assured us that all who seek will find. May those who seek your holiness experience the peace of your Spirit. In your name we ask:

Christ Jesus, you are everywhere through hiddenness and compassion. May we recognize you in the least brother or sister. In your name we ask:

Presider: God of light, we pray as your people in Christ. Help us to set our hearts on the greater gifts, as did St. Scholastica, and come to the banquet of life. We ask this in Jesus' name.

Our Lady of Lourdes (World Day of the Sick, February 11)

Presider: As we celebrate God's healing love in this eucharist, let us be mindful of all whose days are marked by sickness and debility.

Petition Leader: Our response today is, **"God, may our prayer rise to you."**

Christ bore our sufferings so that all may be healed. May the healing power of Christ in the Spirit restore health to all the sick. We pray:

Christ is the consolation of God who heals the broken-hearted. May the prayers of his Mother bring comfort to those afflicted in body, mind, or spirit. We pray:

Mary once shared the mystery of pain at the cross of Christ. May all who are in pain and distress experience her loving protection. We pray:

At Lourdes Mary revealed herself as God's new creation. May Christians who have put on a new humanity through baptism be instruments of healing. We pray:

Mary hastened to be of service to Elizabeth. May all who hasten to healing shrines, especially those that honor Mary, experience Christ's compassion. We pray:

Mary uses her voice in the reign of heaven to advocate for the world's peace. May we use our voices on earth to advocate justice for the sick and financially poor. We pray:

Presider: God, our eyes look hopefully to you to bring us healing and peace in time of sickness. Hear our prayers and strengthen our faith that we may be willing to share in the cross of Christ, through whom we have plenteous redemption. Grant this through Christ, our Lord.

Chair of Peter, Apostle (February 22)

Presider: Let us summon the Spirit of God to sustain the Catholic church in unity and peace through the teaching ministry of the Bishop of Rome.

Petition Leader: Our response is, **"Spirit of unity, be with us."**

Bless abundantly the apostolic ministry of Pope [*Name*] and the church's bishops that the people of God may be built up in love. Trusting in your guidance we pray:

Through the intercession and protection of Mary, Seat of Wisdom, may the Catholic church throughout the world flourish in wisdom and grace. Trusting in your guidance we pray:

May every Christian household be filled with the best spiritual gifts that dignify family life and strengthen the faith of each member. Trusting in your guidance we pray:

Preserve in the church's theologians and catechists a dedication to the truths of faith that serve the well-being of Christian communities. Trusting in your guidance we pray:

Uphold in all priests, deacons, and lay ministers a desire to be of service to the gospel of reconciliation for the good of the faithful. Trusting in your guidance we pray:

Bring to fulfillment the commitment of the church's religious and strengthen them in their respective apostolates. Trusting in your guidance we pray:

Keep alive in the hearts of all the followers of Christ a desire to be united in one faith with one Shepherd praising God at the one table of life. Trusting in your guidance we pray:

Presider: Loving God, by the grace of your Spirit and the intercession of St. Peter, preserve the church in unity and peace through the ministry of Pope [*Name*]. We ask this through Christ, our Teacher and Redeemer.

Bl. Katharine Drexel (March 3)

May the eucharistic presence of Christ that sustained Blessed Katharine Drexel in her service to God and neighbor also animate us to act with compassion and generosity to the least of our sisters and brothers. We pray:

[Also see "Any Saint or Blessed," pages 170-171.]

St. Frances of Rome (March 9)

May the prayers and example of St. Frances of Rome help us to rise above any personal grief so that we may be instruments of God's compassion in the lives of others. We pray:

[Also see "Any Saint or Blessed," pages 170-171.]

St. Patrick (March 17)

May the intercession of St. Patrick bring forth a harvest of peace and unity in Ireland and a renewed dedication among all Christians to pursue the way of love. We pray:

[Also see "Any Saint or Blessed," pages 170-171.]

Solemnity of Joseph, Husband of Mary (March 19)

Presider: Let us pray in the Spirit of faith that blessed the life of Joseph.

Petition Leader: Our response is, **"Christ Jesus, receive our prayer!"**

God established a covenant of faith with Abraham and Sarah; may the church be fortified by the example of the blessed men and women of Israel who trusted God's word, we pray:

God confirmed a covenant of hope with David; may we, like St. Joseph, be mindful of God's enduring promise of salvation to Israel, we pray:

God has given the world Jesus Christ as the covenant of mercy for sinners; may the church embrace God's gift as St. Joseph embraced the Word-Made-Flesh, we pray:

God has called husbands and wives to live a covenant of love; may the intercession of St. Joseph bring blessings to their households, we pray:

God, the Holy Spirit, is given as first fruit of the new covenant; may the church's religious orders dedicated to St. Joseph be filled with the Spirit's gifts, we pray:

God, in Christ, has promised to fulfill all covenants in the city of joy; may the prayers of St. Joseph strengthen the hope of the dying, we pray:

Presider: God of our ancestors, of Joseph and Mary, you have revealed your saving love from the beginning of time. Increase our faith in the covenant of redemption you made with us in Christ, born of Mary, the wife of Joseph. We pray through Christ, our Savior.

Annunciation of the Lord (March 25)[+]

Presider: In Christ, the Word-Made-Flesh, God's kindness is forever established among the children of earth. Let us pray that our fidelity to Christ's word will establish us forever in heaven.

Petition Leader: Our response is, **"Christ Emmanuel, hear our prayer."**

In the Word-Made-Flesh, our humanity has been embraced by God; may we strive with loving hearts to always embrace the divine will. We pray:

In the Word-Made-Flesh, God's steadfast love has been enfleshed; may we enflesh Christ's mercy to those who suffer in body, mind, and spirit. We pray:

In the Word-Made-Flesh, sinners are reconciled to God; may our baptismal consecration to Christ lead others to the wellspring of mercy. We pray:

In the Word-Made-Flesh, the glory of God is shown among us; may we constantly seek to renew all humanity by the grace and peace of the Holy Spirit. We pray:

In the Word-Made-Flesh, a new covenant has been established for all peoples; may our covenant with Christ inspire us to work for greater healing among enemies. We pray:

In the Word-Made-Flesh, we are shown the way to eternal joy; may our communion with Christ in his body and blood lead us to everlasting life. We pray:

Presider: Loving God, whose mercy is everlasting, in the incarnation of your Eternal Word humanity has been given a lasting hope. Hear our prayers and may our lives faithfully reflect the mystery of your presence among us, through Christ, our Lord.

[+] Reprinted from *Graciously Hear Us: General Intercessions for Cycles A, B, and C,* Neil J. Draves-Arpaia, 1998, Ave Maria Press, p. 117.

St. John Baptist de la Salle (April 7)

Presider: Christ, the Teacher, has shown us that humble service befits the reign of heaven. Let us pray for all who serve human flourishing through education.

Petition Leader: Our response today is, **"Saving God, receive our prayer."**

For the church that it may serve the reign of heaven by its commitments to improve the quality of life for all peoples. We pray:

For educational programs that provide technical skills and vocational training, that they may continuously help persons who seek meaningful employment. We pray:

For those who serve as teachers in medical and nursing schools, may they also uphold the sanctity of life before those aspiring to the healing professions. We pray:

For Christian educators of youth (particularly the Brothers of the Christian Schools), may their commitment to teaching be rooted in their faith in the gospel as was that of St. John Baptist de la Salle. We pray:

For all who educate for justice and peace, may their efforts to help free others from poverty and oppression find support in the intercession of St. John Baptist de la Salle. We pray:

For those who teach by their example of virtuous living, especially parents of young children, may they be instruments of the Spirit in the lives of others. We pray:

Presider: God, you call us to be workers, for indeed only one is our Teacher and Messiah, Jesus, your Son. Hear us, we pray, and through the intercession of St. John Baptist de la Salle may those who are dedicated to educational ministries be guided in Spirit and truth. We pray in Jesus' name.

St. Catherine of Siena (April 29)

Presider: With confidence in God's love, let us pray for the grace and peace of the Holy Spirit.

Petition Leader: Our response today is, **"Christ, may your Spirit be with us."**

For the gift of peacemaking; may the Holy Spirit accomplish in our lives the work of unifying factions, particularly within the household of the church. We pray:

For a greater willingness to care for the sick; may our hearts discern the presence of Christ in our brothers and sisters who are ill, particularly where there is prolonged sickness. We pray:

For all engaged in prison ministry; may this work of mercy flourish through the prayers of Catherine of Siena, who served prisoners condemned to death. We pray:

For persons whose spiritual gifts are misunderstood; may the example of Catherine and the strength of the Holy Spirit enable them to bear wrongs patiently. We pray:

For a deeper union with Christ through the gift of prayer; may our lives be enriched by the Spirit of the world's crucified and risen Savior. We pray:

Presider: Christ Jesus, may we who raise our voices in prayer know the blessing of your Spirit, who sanctified the life and work of St. Catherine of Siena for the glory of your name, for you live and reign forever and ever.

Bl. Marie of the Incarnation (April 30, Canada)

May God grant us, through the intercession of Blessed Marie of the Incarnation, a ready and willing love that enfleshes anew the love of Christ. We pray:

[Also see "Any Saint or Blessed," pages 170-171.]

St. Joseph the Worker (May 1)

May we be encouraged by the prayers of St. Joseph for using our talents and gifts to build a better world to God's honor and glory. We pray:

[Also see "Any Saint or Blessed," pages 170-171, or "Blessing of Human Labor," page 187.]

Bl. François Laval (May 6, Canada)

May the dedication and faith of Blessed François Laval encourage bishops of our own time in their ministry of building up the body of Christ, the church. We pray:

[Also see "Any Saint or Blessed," pages 170-171.]

Sts. Isidore and Maria, Farmers (May 15)

May all who harvest the land find in Sts. Isidore and Maria the trusting faith and generous love that are the choice fruits of the Spirit. We pray:

[Also see "Any Saint or Blessed," pages 170-171, or "Blessing of Human Labor," page 187. The petition "For Productive Land," page 211, may also be used on this day.]

St. Philip Neri (May 26)

Presider: Gifted by the Holy Spirit, St. Philip Neri helped to reconcile sinners to Christ. Let us pray that we may also be instruments of God's enduring kindness.

Petition Leader: Our response today is, **"Make us instruments of your mercy, Lord."**

For all who are called to proclaim the good news; may the church's ministry of word and sacrament fan into flame the Spirit's gifts of faith, hope, and love. We pray:

For spiritual mentors and retreat directors; may they be endowed with gifts that help the lives of God's people to bear spiritual fruit. We pray:

For all who minister to pilgrims at shrines and sacred places; may they, like St. Philip Neri, be blessed in extending Christ-like hospitality to others. We pray:

For ourselves gathered to be nourished on the bread of God's Word; may the eucharistic presence of Christ enable us to grow rich in the works of mercy. We pray:

[The following petition may be added where appropriate.]
For the Congregation of the Oratory which St. Philip raised up; may they continue in the good works that Christ inspires. We pray:

For all the dead who placed their trust in God's enduring kindness; may they have everlasting life in the heavenly city (especially _____). We pray:

Presider: God, Fountain of life and holiness, receive our prayers, and by the intercession of your confessor, St. Philip Neri, may we, too, give vibrant witness to Christ in our public lives. Grant our prayers through Christ, our Bread of Life.

Feast of the Visitation (May 31)

Presider: Remembering the great things God has done for us in Christ, let us pray in the Spirit that marked the lives of Mary and Elizabeth.

Petition Leader: Our response today is, **"Redeeming God, hear us."**

We ask God's blessing upon all who carry the good news throughout the world. May the church's work of evangelization flower to God's honor and glory. With joy we call out:

We ask God's blessing upon all who place their lives in service of others. May those who are generous with their love be fortified by grace. With joy we call out:

We ask God's blessing upon all pregnant women. May the Holy Spirit, the Giver of Life, safeguard them and the new life they carry. With joy we call out:

We ask God's blessing upon Catholic health-care ministries and social services. May these works be instruments of God's love in the lives of others. With joy we call out:

We ask God's blessing upon mothers. May the love they give to their households be a sign of God's love for the household of the church. With joy we call out:

We ask God's blessing upon the church as it receives Christ, the Word of Life, in the eucharist. May we experience the strength of the Spirit's grace as did Mary and Elizabeth. With joy we call out:

Presider: God, truly your works are wonderful and great. Receive our prayers and praise on this joyful feast through Christ, our Redeemer.

St. Charles Lwanga and Companions, Martyrs of Uganda (June 3)

Presider: Let us pray for a deepening of the faith that sustained the Ugandan martyrs.

Petition Leader: Our prayer response today is, **"Christ, uphold your servants."**

For all who suffer for the faith especially in environments hostile toward Christianity. Relying on God's love, we ask:

For Pope [*Name*] and all bishops as they work to proclaim the gospel of peace among the faithful. Relying on God's love, we ask:

For catechists who are called to cultivate the Word of Truth in those preparing for baptism. Relying on God's love, we ask:

For native lay Christian leaders in the foreign missions as they encourage their brothers and sisters in their fidelity to Christ. Relying on God's love, we ask:

For peacekeeping missions in their efforts to promote healing in countries torn apart by ethnic and religious rivalries. Relying on God's love, we ask:

For families and religious communities as they mourn the deaths of their sisters and brothers through martyrdom. Relying on God's love, we ask:

Presider: God, hear our prayers. May all who are united to Christ in his suffering find consolation through the prayers of the Ugandan martyrs and come to share in the resurrection of the just. We ask this in Jesus' name.

St. Anthony of Padua (June 13)

Presider: Let us pray that our hearts will remain open to the cries of the poor as was the heart of St. Anthony of Padua.

Petition Leader: Our response today is, **"God, our Help, hear us."**

For the church as it labors to relieve human misery and address its causes, we ask in faith:

For Catholic preachers of the gospel that their message will promote healing and reconciliation under the patronage of St. Anthony, we ask in faith:

For leaders of cities as they seek ways to decrease violence and crime for the good of all, we ask in faith:

For any who are held captive by financial debt, especially poorer nations, we ask in faith:

For charitable organizations and gift-giving programs that generously give to the economically poor, we ask in faith:

For the spiritual good of all who seek God's help through the intercession of St. Anthony, we ask in faith:

Presider: Gracious God, we rely on your saving power to help us. Through the prayers of your servant, St. Anthony, may your people be sustained in faith and hope until all is made new in Christ, our Savior.

St. Aloysius Gonzaga (June 21)

Presider: We turn to God our healer for strength and blessing.

Petition Leader: Our response today will be a moment of silent prayer. [Petition leader, please allow for a sufficient pause after each intercession.]

For any who suffer from AIDS or AIDS-related illnesses.

For all who work with contagious or communicable diseases.

For persons who know life-long debility and poor health.

For blessings upon medical researchers as they strive to find effective immunizations against deadly diseases.

For youth that they may advance in the way of Christ under the prayerful care of St. Aloysius.

For children and youth who are terminally ill.

Presider: God of mercy, hear our prayers. Uphold your servants with a confident faith that our works of love and compassion are pleasing in your sight. We ask this in the name of the compassionate Christ.

Birth of John the Baptist (June 24)

Presider: The child was called John, a name that means "God is gracious." Let us ask God to help us be faithful witnesses of this gracious love revealed in Christ.

Petition Leader: Our response is: **"Gracious God, hear our prayer."**

May our words and actions help point the way to Christ's healing love. We pray:

May the wisdom of the Church's teachings inspire all nations to work for greater justice on the earth. We pray:

May we recognize the Spirit's voice speaking through the prophets of our time, especially those who call us away from all violence. We pray:

May each person be filled with personal gratitude and self-respect for having been wonderfully made by God. We pray:

May the Spirit enlighten us to our continuous need for personal conversion. We pray:

May God sustain us through periods of discouragement in promoting gospel values in our consumer culture. We pray:

Presider: God in heaven, John pointed the way to your gracious love enfleshed in the Lamb of God. Hear our prayers, for we desire to do likewise in the strength of faith. Grant this in Jesus' name.

Sts. Peter and Paul, Apostles (June 29)

Presider: On this feast of the holy apostles let us ask for the Spirit that enabled them to proclaim Christ in life and in death.

Petition Leader: Our response is, **"Keep us strong in faith, O God."**

As we take up the issues and concerns that influence our living the gospel both now and in the future, we pray:

As we, like St. Paul, bring the gospel to peoples of diverse cultures and ways of life, we pray:

As we, like St. Peter, encounter opposition to proclaiming the gospel of life in hostile environments, we pray:

As we strive to carry on the renewal envisioned by the Second Vatican Council, we pray:

As church leadership continues to engage in ecumenical dialogue among Christian churches, we pray:

As the bishops of the United States collaborate with governments and civic agencies in securing justice for the poor, we pray:

As we work to build our parishes into inclusive communities of faith that welcome each person's giftedness, we pray:

Presider: Loving God, in Christ you have formed a new person from old divisions. Saints Peter and Paul ministered to this mystery through their preaching and ministry. Hear our prayers and enable our faith to serve your loving designs. We pray through Christ, our Lord.

Bl. Junipero Serra (July 1)

May the selfless dedication of Blessed Junipero Serra to bring others to faith in Christ inspire all who work in our time to make Christ known throughout the world. We pray:

[Also see "Any Saint or Blessed," pages 170-171.]

St. Benedict (July 11)

Presider: Let us pray that the Spirit of God will lead us in every good path.

Petition Leader: Our prayer response is, **"God of light, send us your Spirit."**

We ask for the Spirit's gift of prayer that the church may continuously contemplate God's word and live by its truth. In faith we call out:

We seek the Spirit's grace for all who labor that the work of our hands and minds will lead to deeper intimacy with Christ. In faith we call out:

We ask today for the gift of wise counsel for leaders of religious communities that their service may encourage holiness and unity. In faith we call out:

We seek the Spirit's joy for any whose hearts are burdened by scruples or anxiety. In faith we call out:

We ask the Spirit to sustain in peace and love the many Benedictine communities throughout the world. In faith we call out:

We seek the Holy Spirit's consolation for all who are in periods of spiritual darkness and uncertainty. In faith we call out:

We entrust to the Spirit of life our beloved dead who sought God's mercy, that they my find in Christ the fulfillment of their hope (especially _____). In faith we call out:

Presider: God in heaven, hear our prayers and hasten to show us your love. Through the intercession of St. Benedict may we use wisely the blessings you send us that all may come to life in Christ, our Light.

Bl. Kateri Tekakwitha (July 14)

Presider: Let us uphold in prayer all who seek to live in God's love.

Petition Leader: Our prayer response is, **"God, receive our prayer."**

God, Source of all life, through the prayers of Blessed Kateri uphold in your peace the native peoples of our land and guide them by your Spirit. With faith in your love, we ask:

God, Redeeming Word, re-create all humanity by your gospel that peoples of every race, culture, and language may dwell in your light. With faith in your love, we ask:

God, sustaining Spirit, give strength to all who experience rejection from their loved ones because of their love for Christ. With faith in your love, we ask:

God, Trinity of Love, watch over those who must flee from abusive circumstances in order to safeguard their faith and dignity. With faith in your love, we ask:

God, our beginning and end, fill each Christian community with compassionate love for persons who seek safe refuge among us. With faith in your love, we ask:

God, our Help in time of trial, sustain us in your grace that our lives may reflect the simplicity and holiness of Blessed Kateri. With faith in your love, we ask:

Presider: Loving God, your care reaches all the peoples of the earth. Hear our prayers and help us always to be channels of your love, especially to those most in need. Grant this through Christ, our Redeemer.

St. Mary Magdalene (July 22)

Presider: Christ sent St. Mary Magdalene as an apostle to the apostles with the good news of the resurrection. Let us pray that we will be faithful heralds of the same life-giving message.

Petition Leader: Our response today is, **"Risen Savior, hear our prayer."**

For the church entrusted with the gospel of life, that it may act on the word it has received in faith. We call on Christ and pray:

For a greater openness and affirmation of the spiritual gifts of church women as they carry the gospel of peace to God's people. We call on Christ and pray:

For all the baptized, that we may live in fidelity to the Holy Spirit who fashions us to be a new creation in Christ. We call on Christ and pray:

For those who grieve the loss of loved ones, that they may be consoled by the Word of Life, who is Jesus Christ. We call on Christ and pray:

For all who seek to know and encounter God's liberating love, that the Spirit of truth and healing will lead them by the light of faith. We call on Christ and pray:

For our deceased brothers and sisters, that they may rejoice at the banquet of life in the company of St. Mary Magdalene (especially _____). We call on Christ and pray:

Presider: Redeeming God, graciously listen to the sound of our call. May we who have received the good news through the witness of St. Mary Magdalene be moved to praise your goodness to us in Christ, our risen Savior.

Sts. Joachim and Ann (July 26)

Presider: Let us invoke the Holy Spirit to strengthen us in living our covenant of faith in the blood of Christ.

Petition Leader: Our prayer response today is, **"God, pour out your Spirit."**

May God, who promised Abraham and Sarah many descendants through faith, uphold in grace all who trust in God's promise of new life. We pray:

May God, who announced to David an everlasting reign of peace, strengthen the faith of all who have been anointed to be a priestly people. We pray:

May God, who has spoken to us through the prophets, bless the work of all Bible scholars and teachers of the gospel. We pray:

May God, who led Israel from slavery, continue to free all who are held bound by sin and oppression. We pray:

[In Canada only:]
May God, who fashioned a new people in Christ, guide the leaders and peoples of Canada, entrusted to the patronage of St. Ann. We pray:

May God, who raised Jesus from the dead, bestow eternal life to all who relied on God's covenant of mercy (especially_____). We pray:

Presider: God of our ancestors and Abba of Jesus, hear our prayers, for we trust in the covenant of love you have decreed in the resurrection of Christ. May we live its command of love and peace all our days. We ask this in the name of Jesus, born of Mary.

St. Martha (July 29)

Presider: Let us remember in prayer the labors of love that are undertaken in a spirit of generosity and care.

Petition Leader: Our prayer response today is, **"God, hear our prayer."**

We implore God to grace the lives of all homemakers. May God send blessing, we pray:

We entrust to God's care all who work as volunteers in soup kitchens and food pantries. May God send blessing, we pray:

We raise up in prayer all who freely devote their time as mentors for people learning English as a second language. May God send blessing, we pray:

We place in God's hands those who work as emergency medical technicians, volunteer firefighters, and rescue teams. May God send blessing, we pray:

We rely on God to sustain persons who offer support to the terminally ill and their families as hospice aids and volunteers. May God send blessing, we pray:

We ask God to guide adults who serve as Big Brothers/Big Sisters, Boy and Girl Scout leaders, or in Catholic youth ministries. May God send blessing, we pray:

We place before God all who give of themselves through support group services, especially to the grieving. May God send blessing, we pray:

Presider: God, whatever we do, whether at work or leisure, may we do in the name of Christ and a spirit of love. Hear our prayers, united to the intercession of St. Martha of Bethany, and bless the work of our hands. We ask this in the name of Jesus.

St. Ignatius Loyola (July 31)

Presider: Let us pray that the love and grace of God will be our sustenance as we journey in faith.

Petition Leader: Our prayer response today is, **"Lord, give us your love and grace."**

For the church as it shares its spiritual treasures with all who seek to discern God's will, we pray:

For God's people who enter a time of retreat and prayerful reflection, we pray:

For Catholic colleges, universities, and spirituality centers, we pray:

For all who serve God's people as theologians, spiritual directors, and military chaplains, we pray:

For persons who are in periods of religious conversion and renewal, we pray:

For persons who have vowed to respect life in a culture of death, we pray:

[The following petition may be added where appropriate.]
For the members of the Society of Jesus, their associates, and Jesuit Volunteer Corps, we pray:

Presider: God in heaven, hear our prayers on this feast of St. Ignatius Loyola. With your love and grace, so freely given, may we advance in holiness of life. Grant this through Christ, our Savior.

St. Alphonsus Liguori (August 1)

Presider: Christ, our Redeemer, has triumphed over sin and death. With grateful hearts let us invoke the Savior's name for the life of the world.

Petition Leader: Our prayer response today is, **"Christ, our Redeemer, hear us."**

For the people of God in Christ, may the church advance toward the reign of God as a united household of faith. Rejoicing in God's love, we call out:

For all who serve in the church as moral theologians and ethicists, under the patronage of St. Alphonsus may their work help all to fulfill the love command of Christ. Rejoicing in God's love, we call out:

For persons who are discouraged and depressed by failure and rejection, may the Spirit of Christ renew their strength and vitality. Rejoicing in God's love, we call out:

For all who are engaged in preaching missions, may their proclamation of God's love bring many to Christ, the wellspring of mercy. Rejoicing in God's love, we call out:

For those who work to alleviate poverty and its effects, may their works of mercy prosper through the intercession of St. Alphonsus. Rejoicing in God's love, we call out:

[The following petition may be added where appropriate.]
For the Redemptorist Fathers and Brothers, may the Spirit continue to fill them with the grace that sanctified the life of their founder, St. Alphonsus. Rejoicing in God's love, we call out:

For the dead who believed that in Christ there is plenteous redemption, may they find light and life in the reign of heaven (especially _____). Rejoicing in God's love, we call out:

Presider: God in heaven, indeed we rejoice in your saving love. May we, who pray in the name of Jesus, be filled with the enduring love of your Word-Made-Flesh. Grant this through Christ, our Redeemer.

St. John Vianney (August 4)

Presider: Called by Christ to be a priestly people, let us seek the grace of God that strengthens us for living a Christian life.

Petition Leader: Our prayer response today is, **"God of mercy, hear us."**

For the church, which St. John Vianney served as a humble priest, may it abide in the peace and love of Jesus Christ. We pray:

For those who serve God's people as parish priests, may the example and prayers of the Curé of Ars help them to fulfill their ministry with gentleness and dedication. We pray:

For students who struggle with learning difficulties as did St. John Vianney, may they not give in to discouragement and continue with complete confidence in God's power. We pray:

For farmers and any who labor close to the land, may their work bring forth food for our tables and their faith the fruit of love. We pray:

For Christians who are alienated from the love of Christ because of sin, may the Spirit prompt them to be reconciled through the sacraments of the church. We pray:

For ourselves who feast on the Bread of Life, may we cultivate with God's help lives that are rich in faith, hope, and love. We pray:

For any who are considering a vocation to the diocesan priesthood or religious life, may the Spirit guide their discernment. We pray:

Presider: God, receive our prayers for your life-giving grace and peace. Through the intercession of St. John Vianney may we hold fast to your blessings, persevere in prayer, and come to the table of life in your kingdom. We pray in Jesus' name.

St. Dominic (August 8)

Presider: Jesus promised that the Spirit of truth would guide the church. Let us pray for the light of the Spirit on this feast of St. Dominic.

Petition Leader: Our response is, **"Christ, send forth your light."**

Believing that God is the Creator of heaven and earth, may we use the Spirit's gifts to live reverently and justly as we await the day of Christ. We pray:

Believing that Christ is truly God, may the Catholic church, strengthened by the prayers of St. Dominic, joyfully proclaim the gospel that gives light to all peoples. We pray:

Believing that Christ is truly human, may all believers live in accord with the new humanity put on in baptism. We pray:

Believing that the Holy Spirit spoke through the prophets, may we, like St. Dominic, use our voices to advocate for justice. We pray:

Believing that Christ abides among us in word and sacrament, may all who receive these gifts in faith be fortified in their love for God. We pray:

[The following petition may be added where appropriate.]
Believing that God brings all things to perfection in Christ, may the world-wide Dominican family continue to joyfully announce the good news in word and deed. We pray:

Believing that Christ has triumphed over death, may all the dead rise to the glory of the resurrection on the last day (especially _____). We pray:

Presider: God, hear us as we invoke the grace of your Spirit. May we live as your holy people and come to share the joy of St. Dominic and the saints in light. Grant our prayers in Jesus' name.

St. Clare of Assisi (August 11)

Presider: Christ called blessed those who are poor in spirit. Let us pray that all may find their lasting wealth in Christ.

Petition Leader: Our prayer response today is a moment of silent prayer after each petition. [Petition leader, please allow for a sufficient pause after each intercession.]

Christ made himself poor that we may be rich in love for God and neighbor. May all Christians be filled with the same generous love.

Christ assured us that humankind does not live on bread alone. May the bread of God's word sustain our faith, hope, and love.

St. Clare chose to be poor that Christ alone might be her wealth. May her prayers help us to live simply and trustfully in God's unending care for all creation.

St. Clare committed her life to vigilant prayer. May the same Holy Spirit who graced her life uphold in us the gift of persevering prayer, especially in time of difficulty.

Wisdom has prepared her table that all may feast on God's loving kindness. May the Spirit lead many hearts to feast on the eucharistic presence of Christ.

[The following petition may be added where appropriate.]
St. Clare lived as a city of light in a darkened world. May the Spirit of light continue to bless the lives of the Poor Clares throughout the world.

The Spirit, who raised Jesus from the dead, has been poured into our hearts. May the dead who lived by the Spirit of Christ find everlasting joy in heaven (especially _____).

Presider: God, you alone are our lasting joy. In your goodness listen to us asking for your grace. Through the prayers of St. Clare may your church courageously live its faith and be ready to meet Christ, your Beloved, on the last day. We ask this in the name of Jesus, the risen Savior.

St. Maximilian Kolbe (Aug. 14)

Presider: Let us pray.

Petition Leader: Our prayer response today is, **"Lord, hear our prayer."**

Christ is the way that leads to eternal life. May the church vigorously pursue the way of love, revealed in Christ, even in the face of persecution. We humbly ask:

Christ is our truth. May the Spirit working through the church win the hearts and minds of persons who build structures of hate. We humbly ask:

Christ is our life. May God's protection be with all who labor at great personal risk to eliminate violence to human life. We humbly ask:

Christ is our peace. May St. Maximilian intercede for the conversion of Christians who are alienated from Christ by their hatred. We humbly ask:

Christ called blessed those who weep and mourn. May the consoling Spirit uphold races and religions that know the pain of mass killings. We humbly ask:

Christ, at the hour of his death, entrusted his Mother to St. John. At the hour of our death may the Mother of God entrust us to Christ. We humbly ask:

Presider: God of peace, receive our prayers as we recall the life and death of your faithful servant, St. Maximilian. Joined to Christ through faith and martyrdom he has found lasting peace in your presence. May we arrive at the same joy when our life's journey is ended. Grant this through Christ, our Redeemer.

St. Bernard (August 20)

Presider: Mindful of God's unending love for the church, let us pray that God's Spirit will continue to guide us.

Petition Leader: Our prayer response is, **"Spirit of God, guide us."**

God, send your Spirit of holiness upon the leaders of the Catholic church, Pope [*Name*] and bishops, that their ministry may foster unity within your people. We pray in faith:

God, pour out your Spirit of love upon abbots and abbesses that like St. Bernard they may serve with wisdom and understanding. We pray in faith:

God, fill with the Spirit's wise counsel all who work as negotiators for peace that through the intercession and example of St. Bernard nations may live in harmony. We pray in faith:

God, sustain by the Spirit's power all who are consecrated to you in monastic religious life that they may enrich your household of faith with the gift of their lives. We pray in faith:

[The following petition may be added where appropriate.]
God, bless abundantly the church's Cistercian communities, which build on St. Bernard's legacy, that they may flourish in faith, hope, and love. We pray in faith:

God, inspire us, as you did St. Bernard, with a genuine love for the Mother of God that through her protection and prayers we may be filled with the Spirit of Christ. We pray in faith:

Presider: Loving God, you fill your household of faith with an array of spiritual gifts. Hear our prayers for your Spirit that we may honor you always, like St. Bernard, with our praise and our actions, through Christ, our Savior.

St. Pius X (August 21)

Presider: Let us entrust to God the life of the church.

Petition Leader: Our prayer response today is, **"God of mercy, hear us."**

For the Catholic church, which St. Pius X served as universal pastor; may it always live as a light to the nations and a sign of unity. Trusting in God's care, we ask:

For Pope [*Name*]; may the ministry of the Bishop of Rome foster harmony in the universal church and a deepening of love for Jesus Christ. Trusting in God's care, we ask:

For the Archdiocese/Diocese of _____ and Archbishop/Bishop [*Name*]; may the life of Christ we share in faith and love flourish to the glory of God. Trusting in God's care, we ask:

For the faithful of Christ, that the Spirit of truth will lead all believers to cherish the love of God revealed in Jesus and the teaching of the apostles. Trusting in God's care, we ask:

For the church's theological commissions as they address issues of our times; may they be guided by the Spirit's wisdom and the vision of Vatican Council II. Trusting in God's care, we ask:

For groups that have ceased to be in communion with the Catholic church; may the prayers of St. Pius X and the work of the Holy Spirit bring forth reconciliation. Trusting in God's care, we ask:

For children and adults who are preparing for first eucharist, may the Spirit's gifts of knowledge and understanding be with them as they approach the table of life. Trusting in God's care, we ask:

Presider: Compassionate God, guide your church always, we humbly ask. By the power of your Spirit lead your faithful people in Christ by the light of one faith and one hope until we rejoice in your presence forever. Grant this in Jesus' name.

St. Rose of Lima (August 23)

May the prayers of St. Rose of Lima and her example of hiddenness inspire in the lives of the peoples of the Americas a greater love for simplicity, humility, and reverence for God. We pray:

[Also see "Any Saint or Blessed," pages 170-171.]

St. Monica (August 27)

Presider: Today let our intercessory prayers invoke God's grace for our families.

Petition Leader: Our prayer response is, **"Gracious God, hear us."**

We entrust to God's care families that are afflicted by drug or substance abuse. Through the prayers of St. Monica and God's grace may sobriety prevail. With confident faith we ask:

We invoke God's sustaining love to uphold persons in recovery from substance or drug abuse. May personal prayer and the grace of the sacraments be their sources of strength. With confident faith we ask:

We join our voices with parents praying for the conversion of their children who have abandoned Christianity. May they draw courage from the example of St. Monica. With confident faith we ask:

We intercede for all Christian wives and mothers. May they be blessed with a strong faith and love and their homes filled with the light of Christ. With confident faith we ask:

We ask God to uphold all families, regardless of creed. May the Spirit grace families with every spiritual gift, especially those members who are ill. With confident faith we ask:

Presider: God, in your kindness hear our prayers. Through the intercession of St. Monica and the grace of Christ, may families live in peace and know your saving love, through Christ, our Redeemer.

St. Augustine (August 28)

Presider: Let us pray that all will come to know the one God, a Trinity of Persons, and be filled with the divine life.

Petition Leader: Our response today is, **"Loving God, hear our prayer."**

God, our Creator, you have willed our salvation in Christ. Bless us with a strong faith in your will and the grace to fulfill it. We ask:

God, our Redeemer, you have dwelt among us in Jesus Christ, the Incarnate Word. Sustain in us a love for your revealed Word and the grace to follow Christ. We ask:

God, our Sanctifier, you give us new life in Christ. May your indwelling presence lead us all to truth and enable us to live as sons and daughters of God. We ask:

God, Trinity of Persons, endow your church with a love for the sacramental life that we may share your intimacy in the reign of heaven. We ask:

God, abounding in kindness and mercy, by your grace and the intercession of St. Augustine may all peoples be reborn at the font of new life. We ask:

God, Source of all wisdom and peace, pour forth your reconciling Spirit upon the hearts and minds of all Christians that the followers of Christ may live in unity. We ask:

Presider: God in heaven, hear our prayers. Through the teachings and prayers of St. Augustine may your church advance in wisdom and understanding of the gospel of our salvation. Grant this in Jesus' name.

Beheading of John the Baptist (August 29)

Presider: Let us pray.

Petition Leader: Our response is, **"Lord, hear our prayer."**

For the church called to share in the prophetic ministry of Christ, that it will faithfully proclaim the Word of Life in its fullness. We ask in faith:

For those who suffer persecution for what is right and just, that they may be fortified by the Holy Spirit. We ask in faith:

For leaders of nations and heads of state, that their private lives and public service will be marked by the highest ethical standards. We ask in faith:

For ourselves as we receive the Word of Life this day, that we may be strengthened to give witness to Christ at all times. We ask in faith:

For those who met death by violence for their commitment to God's truth, that they may rejoice with St. John the Baptist in the reign of heaven. We ask in faith:

Presider: Life-giving God, hear our prayers, and by your grace may we live the truths we celebrate in Word and sacrament. Grant this through Christ, the Lord.

St. Peter Claver (September 9)

Presider: Remembering that we are a priestly people gathered to Christ from every race, language, and culture, let us pray in the one Spirit.

Petition Leader: Our response today is, **"Christ Jesus, hear our prayer."**

For an end to all forms of racism in private and public life, especially among Christians. Called to love as Christ loved, we ask:

For a greater willingness among wealthier nations to help improve the quality of life for all oppressed peoples of the world. Called to love as Christ loved, we ask:

For an outpouring of compassion within our churches for persons afflicted with contagious diseases. Called to love as Christ loved, we ask:

For a deepening of our love for God that we may be united in the Spirit who sanctified the life of St. Peter Claver. Called to love as Christ loved, we ask:

For an increase of openness within our parishes to the diverse gifts of all races and cultures that the universal beauty of the Catholic church may show forth. Called to love as Christ loved, we ask:

Presider: God of love and Creator of all, help us to live always as your people united in the one Spirit. Hear our prayers, come to our aid, and by the prayers of St. Peter Claver may we experience your transforming grace. We ask this in Jesus' name.

St. Andrew Kim Taegon and Martyrs of Korea (September 20)

Presider: The faith of the Korean martyrs remained firm despite persecution and death. Let us pray that their witness will inspire all Christians to remain true to their faith.

Petition Leader: Our response today is, **"God, our Help, hear us."**

May our personal love for Christ abound even when we are subject to ridicule or derision. Trusting in God's love, we pray:

May the Catholic church in Korea, inspired by the spiritual legacy of these martyred men, women, and children, continue to give vibrant witness to Christ. Trusting in God's love, we pray:

May the Spirit of God and the intercession of the Korean martyrs help unify the land of Korea into a single peaceful nation. Trusting in God's love, we pray:

May the efforts of the church and leaders of nations to reduce religious persecution wherever it exists be blessed by God. Trusting in God's love, we pray:

May lay Christian leaders and catechists be endowed with every spiritual gift that faith in Christ may bear fruit among God's people. Trusting in God's love, we pray:

May Christian clergy, religious, and laypersons who have been killed because of their faith and service to the poor rejoice in the company of the Korean martyrs. Trusting in God's love, we pray:

Presider: God of the living and the dead, we glory in the cross of Christ, who is our Life and Salvation. Receive our prayers and enrich our faith through the working of your consoling Spirit. We ask this in Jesus' name.

St. Vincent de Paul (September 27)

Presider: Let us pray that love will be the foundation of our life in Christ, as it was for St. Vincent de Paul.

Petition Leader: Our response today is, **"God, fill us with your love."**

For all who are held hostage by kidnappers and terrorists. May we, like St. Vincent, arrive at forgiveness of those who do us harm. We pray:

For individuals and teams that work to negotiate release of persons unjustly deprived of liberty. May God's liberating love guide their efforts to free persons who are captives of terrorists and oppressive regimes. We pray:

For the church wherever it ministers to persons enslaved by drugs and prostitution. May the Christian community be God's instrument of reconciliation and peace in the lives of others. We pray:

For Catholic health-care systems, social services and charitable societies. May each of these, through St. Vincent's intercession, continue to manifest the compassion of Christ to others. We pray:

For all who are sick among us, especially infants and children. May God's healing Spirit restore health and well-being to all people. We pray:

[The following petition may be added where appropriate.]
For the Vincentian priests and brothers and the Daughters of Charity. May these religious communities, impelled by the love of Christ, flourish in the Spirit who filled St. Vincent. We pray:

For ourselves as we celebrate the eucharistic mystery of Christ. May God's grace enable us to live the life of Christ faithfully. We pray:

Presider: God, fill us with the love of Christ that we may scatter the darkness caused by sin. May we walk always as a people of the light and be instruments of your love in the lives of others as was St. Vincent. We ask this through Christ, our Light and Salvation.

Michael, Gabriel, and Raphael, Archangels (September 29)

Presider: Let us ask the Holy Spirit to sanctify our lives that heaven and earth may be filled with God's glory.

Petition Leader: Our response is, **"Come, Spirit of love!"**

Through the power of the Holy Spirit may we become like Christ and join in St. Michael's joy, we pray:

Through the power of the anointing Spirit may we be agents of healing and join in St. Raphael's adoration, we pray:

Through the power of the sanctifying Spirit may we be strong in love and join in St. Gabriel's praise, we pray:

Through the presence of the Holy Spirit and the prayer ministry of St. Michael may the church be protected from evil, we pray:

Through the light of the Holy Spirit and the prayer ministry of St. Gabriel may the church continue the saving mission of Christ, we pray:

Through the consoling love of the Holy Spirit and the prayer ministry of St. Raphael may the church witness God's mercy to the sick and suffering, we pray:

Through the love the Queen of Angels bears for the church, may the faithful departed be led by her and the archangels into the heavenly city, we pray:

Presider: Saving God, send us your Spirit that we may serve you at all times and be loud in your praise in company with the archangels and saints. Grant this through Jesus Christ, our Mediator and Savior.

St. Jerome (September 30)

Presider: Let us pray that God's word, in all its richness, will direct our steps and inspire all people to love.

Petition Leader: Our prayer response is, **"Christ, Word of God, hear us."**

By God's word, all things were made. May the Holy Spirit continue to inspire in the hearts of the faithful a profound love for the revealed Word. We pray:

By God's word, all things have been reconciled in heaven and earth. May Christ, the Word-Made-Flesh, find a dwelling place in every human heart. We pray:

By the light of the gospel the saints found blessedness. May the light of faith guide to Christ, the font of salvation, all who seek to know God. We pray:

By the bread of God's word, the hungry have been filled with good things. May all who minister God's word and sacraments in the church enjoy the guidance of the Holy Spirit. We pray:

By the wisdom of God's word the church is built up in faith. May the Spirit, who made fruitful the work of St. Jerome, bless the work of Bible scholars and commissions. We pray:

By the power of God's word the faithful departed shall rise to the glory of the resurrection. May all who grieve be consoled by the hope of the gospel of Jesus Christ. We pray:

Presider: God, from the beginning of time you have revealed your love for us. Receive our prayers, and by the love you bear for us in Christ may your church be filled with new life. Grant this in Jesus' name.

St. Thérèse of Lisieux (October 1)

Presider: Let us embrace in prayer the needs of the church and world as we recall the confident faith that sustained St. Thérèse.

Petition Leader: Our response today is, **"Faithful God, hear our prayer."**

For the church, called to share in the one sacrifice of Christ; may every action of the church be rooted in love for God and neighbor. With confident faith we ask:

For the conversion of those most alienated from God; may the grace of the Holy Spirit lead many to be renewed in God's merciful love. With confident faith we ask:

For the gift of simplicity in our daily lives; may our ordinary actions, however small or great, be undertaken in a spirit of love. With confident faith we ask:

For all who experience spiritual darkness and doubt, as did St. Thérèse; may their faith remain firm and constant through the power of God's sustaining Spirit. With confident faith we ask:

For all who know long suffering, especially young people; may the heroic trust of St. Thérèse encourage a lively faith in all who are ill. With confident faith we ask:

For all who serve in the missions as instruments of God's tender mercies; with the help of St. Thérèse's prayers may missionaries be filled with every spiritual blessing. With confident faith we ask:

Presider: Merciful God, you inspire every good intention and bring all things to perfection in Christ. Receive our prayers, fill us with your love, and bring us at last into the reign of heaven where St. Thérèse praises your love eternally through Christ, our Savior.

Guardian Angels (October 2)

Presider: Confident that God's love surrounds us, let us pray that our church and world may abide in peace and safety.

Petition Leader: Our prayer response today is, **"God, bless and keep us."**

For the church, that it may dwell in the security of God's love, especially in cultures hostile to Christianity. We pray:

For our families, that each member, especially our elderly and children, may enjoy God's protection from harm. We pray:

For our elected officials, that they may be kept safe from terrorists and people of violence. We pray:

For all who are traveling, that their journeys will be blessed through the ministry of God's angels and saints. We pray:

For the gift of prayer, that all Christians, filled with the Spirit of love, may be one with the angels in praising God's glory day and night. We pray:

For a deepening of our faith, that we may continue to recognize God's personal love and care for every living creature. We pray:

For the faithful departed, that the angels of God will conduct them into the heavenly Jerusalem. We pray:

Presider: Saving God, may our prayer rise to you through the ministry of your angels. Watch over us always, and may we never cease to praise your goodness through Christ, our Lord.

St. Francis of Assisi (October 4)

Presider: Let us call upon God's Spirit to fill all creation with the glory of the risen Christ.

Petition Leader: Our prayer response is, **"Spirit of peace, be with us."**

As the church labors in the name of Christ crucified, that all may come to know the wideness of God's mercy, we pray:

As world leaders strive to overcome obstacles to world peace, we pray:

As societies undertake programs to preserve natural resources and reduce wastefulness, we pray:

As families work to foster harmony, well-being, and spiritual unity among all members, we pray:

As Christians reach out to the economically poor and sick, as did St. Francis, we pray:

As we read the signs of our times calling all people away from violence and to be instruments of healing and peace, we pray:

[The following petition may be added where appropriate.]
As Franciscan communities throughout the world continue to give vitality to the charism and ministry of their holy founder, Francis, we pray:

As we return to the earth our beloved dead in the sure and certain hope of resurrection (especially _____), we pray:

Presider: God, indeed heaven and earth are full of your glory through the presence of your Spirit. On this memorial of your humble servant, Francis, we call on your redeeming love to fill us with every spiritual blessing. Grant our prayers in the name of Jesus, the Lord.

Bl. Marie-Rose Durocher (October 6)

May the intercession of Blessed Marie-Rose bring spiritual vitality to all who serve to make the gospel of life known and loved, particularly the Sisters of the Holy Names of Jesus and Mary. We pray:

[Also see "Any Saint or Blessed," pages 170-171.]

St. Teresa of Avila (October 15)

Presider: Let us ask Christ to bestow on the church of our time the rich gifts of the Spirit that also filled St. Teresa of Avila.

Petition Leader: Our response today is, **"Gift Divine, fill our hearts."**

Come, Spirit of the living God, bestow on the church, its leaders and faithful, the desire for union with God. We call you forth in the name of Jesus and ask:

Come, Spirit of all wisdom and understanding, grant to the hearts that seek your guidance gifts in keeping with the splendor of Christ. We call you forth in the name of Jesus and ask:

Come, Spirit, Giver of Life, quicken in all the baptized the fires of faith, hope, and love. We call you forth in the name of Jesus and ask:

Come, Spirit of peace, purify every heart of hatred and violence that all may see God. We call you forth in the name of Jesus and ask:

Come, Spirit of truth, abide with all spiritual reformers in the church of our time that the Christian people may dwell in unity and holiness. We call you forth in the name of Jesus and ask:

Come, Spirit, Source of our inspiration, enable us to act on the Word of Life that the poor and sick may be consoled in every trial. We call you forth in the name of Jesus and ask:

[The following petition may be included where appropriate.]
Come, Spirit of love, kindle in the hearts of every Carmelite the fire of love that sanctified the life of St. Teresa. We call you forth in the name of Jesus and ask:

Presider: God in heaven, hear us as we invoke your Spirit in the name of Jesus. May love always be the foundation of our lives that with St. Teresa and the company of saints we may grasp the immensity of your love for us in time and in eternity. Grant our prayer through Christ, our Lord.

St. Marguerite d'Youville (October 16, Canada)

Presider: God gifted St. Marguerite d'Youville with a faith that stood firm in adversity. Let us ask the same Eternal Father, whom Marguerite loved, for every grace and blessing.

Petition Leader: Our response today is, **"Compassionate God, hear our prayer."**

For all who open their hearts and homes to the poor, the orphaned, and the reviled; may they know God's providential care. We pray:

For children who lose a parent at a young age; may their trust in God's eternal care be their protection and consolation. We pray:

For parents who grieve the loss of a child; may they, like St. Marguerite, find God's abiding love a solid source of comfort in their sorrow. We pray:

For any who are ridiculed and insulted because of their commitment to charity and justice for the poor; may the grace of the Holy Spirit, and St. Marguerite's example, be their source of strength. We pray:

For those who suffer the loss of loved ones and property because of fires; may they draw courage and hope from the heart of Christ through the intercession of St. Marguerite. We pray:

[The following petition may be added where appropriate.]
For the communities of compassionate love which St. Marguerite founded; may the Grey Nuns continue to extend the charity and love of Christ to those most in need. We pray:

For all our loved ones who are ill; may the healing power of Christ uphold them in faith and trust. We pray:

Presider: Gracious God, we place our trust in your loving providence. Hasten to help us, we humbly pray, and fill us with every blessing, through Jesus Christ, our Savior.

Sts. Isaac Jogues, Jean de Brébeuf, and Companions, North American Martyrs
(October 19 in the U.S., September 26 in Canada)

Presider: On this feast of the North American martyrs let our prayers express our trust in God's redeeming love.

Petition Leader: Our prayer response is, **"God, graciously hear us."**

Entrusted with the good news of salvation, may the Catholic church in Canada/the United States be filled with the zeal of Sts. Isaac, John, and companions for renewing all things in Christ. With hope-filled joy we pray:

Enriched by the sacraments of new life, may all the baptized provide convincing witness to their personal love for Christ as did these holy martyrs. With hope-filled joy we pray:

Enlivened by the anointing Spirit, may the church's commitment to justice and equality bring all nations together in the peace of Christ. With hope-filled joy we pray:

Endowed with diverse gifts of the Spirit, may each of us act on the grace we are given to be a healing presence in the world. With hope-filled joy we pray:

Enlightened by Christ, may the faithful who proclaim the mystery of faith in this eucharist be strengthened in time of trial. With hope-filled joy we pray:

Embraced by the mercy of God, may all who have fallen asleep in Christ rejoice with the company of the martyrs in the New Jerusalem. With hope-filled joy we pray:

Presider: Redeeming God, we praise the greatness of your love. Hear our prayers, and by the intercession of Sts. Isaac, John, and their companions fill us with a courageous faith. We ask this through Christ, the Lamb who was slain and raised to life.

St. Paul of the Cross (October 19)

May the prayers of St. Paul of the Cross assist the men and women of the Congregation of the Passion and all who daily take up the cross of personal suffering. We pray:

[Also see "Any Saint or Blessed," pages 170-171.]

All Saints (November 1)[+]

Presider: Let us call forth the Holy Spirit that, like the saints, we might be filled with the light of faith and love.

Petition Leader: Our prayer response is: **"Spirit of God, dwell with us."**

May the Holy Spirit fill us with a personal love for God whom we are called to love above all else. We ask in faith:

May the Spirit of truth kindle in our hearts a passion for mercy that we may rejoice in God's mercy on our day of need. We ask in faith:

May the Spirit who raised Jesus from the dead restore life to those who have abandoned faith in Christ. We ask in faith:

May the Comforter stir in us a zeal for justice that renews the face of the earth. We ask in faith:

May the Spirit, our Counselor, be with our youth that their lives will reflect the light of Christ. We ask in faith:

May the Spirit of all grace and peace uphold those who suffer for their commitment to Christ and the gospel of life. We ask in faith:

May the Spirit who sanctified the lives of the saints bring our beloved dead into the reign of light. We ask in faith:

Presider: God of compassion, you have shared the victory of Christ with the saints. Hear our prayers for your Spirit that our lives may be rooted in love and make us worthy to share the joy of the saints. We ask this in Jesus' name.

[+] Reprinted from *Graciously Hear Us: General Intercessions for Cycles, A, B, and C*, Neil J. Draves-Arpaia, 1998, Ave Maria Press, p. 125.

All Souls (Nov. 2)[+]

Presider: The light of Christ's resurrection reveals the immensity of God's mercy. Let us pray that our faith in God's mercy and love be fortified.

Petition Leader: Our response is, **"God of the living and the dead, uphold us."**

When we grieve the loss of those we love, we ask:

When we invoke the saving death of Christ for any who are still deprived of your eternal light, we ask:

When we call on your mercy for those who have died without the consolation of baptism, we ask:

When death is caused by human malice and anger robs us of peace, we ask:

When our faith in your providential care is challenged, we ask:

When terminal illness signals that our earthly pilgrimage is coming to an end, we ask:

When our only consolation is the hope of seeing you face to face, we ask:

Presider: God, rich in compassion, hear our prayers for those who have died. Sustain your pilgrim people in the hope that your promise of mercy reaches all humanity. We ask this through Christ Jesus, the first-born of all the dead.

[+] Reprinted from *Graciously Hear Us: General Intercessions for Cycles A, B, and C*, Neil J. Draves-Arpaia, 1998, Ave Maria Press, p. 126.

St. Martin de Porres (November 3)

Presider: Mindful that God raises the lowly to high places to fill them with every good gift, let us pray assured of St. Martin de Porres' intercession.

Petition Leader: Our response today is, **"Compassionate God, hear us."**

You filled St. Martin de Porres with compassion for the poor and the enslaved. Enable us as well to respond with compassionate love for all who are oppressed by poverty and injustice. We pray:

You empowered Martin to be a faithful steward of your generous love. Help us to be generous in sharing our bread with the hungry and our love with the orphaned. We pray:

You endowed Martin with simple skills which he put to good use. May we use our talents wisely and responsibly in humility and joy. We pray:

You raised up Martin, an interracial son of unwed parents, to be a light of holiness in Peru. By your Spirit of love, and Martin's prayers, scatter the darkness of racism from our midst. We pray:

You gave Martin the wealth of spiritual riches to draw him to yourself. May we recognize the gifts you give to each of us for our eternal good. We pray:

You chose Martin to be an instrument of your consolation to the sick. By his prayers may all who are ill and lonely experience your healing love. We pray:

Presider: All glory and praise to your name, God of mercy. As we call on you to fill us with love, as you did St. Martin, may we never cease to give you thanks through Christ, our risen Savior.

St. Charles Borromeo (November 4)

Presider: Let us embrace in our prayers the spiritual well-being of the church which St. Charles served with total dedication.

Petition Leader: Our prayer response is, **"Christ, renew us through love."**

For the Catholic church throughout the world. Christ, build up each local church to be prophetic, compassionate, and faithful to your word. We pray:

For Pope [*Name*] and bishops. Christ, guide their pastoral ministry that all peoples may hear the universal call to holiness. We pray:

For the clergy. Christ, bestow on all ordained for service the Spirit of loving kindness that marked the life of St. Charles Borromeo. We pray:

For catechists and teachers of the faith. Christ, fill with your Spirit of fidelity those entrusted with the religious education of your people. We pray:

For seminarians. Christ, raise up in your church priestly servants who will be faithful instruments of your compassionate love and redeeming word. We pray:

For all who have fallen away from the faith. Christ, through the prayers of St. Charles and by your reconciling Spirit, renew the grace of baptism in your people. We pray:

Presider: Loving God, sustain your church in the peace and compassion of Jesus Christ. Receive our prayers and keep your household of faith united in love. Grant this in Jesus' name.

Dedication of the Lateran Basilica (November 9)

Presider: We are called to be a fit dwelling place for God in the Spirit. Let us invoke the Spirit of holiness for the good of Christ's church.

Petition Leader: Our response is, **"Spirit of God, dwell with us."**

For the Catholic church, Pope [*Name*], bishop of Rome, and all bishops, that their ministry of preaching and teaching may be guided by the Spirit of truth. We pray:

For all the baptized, that the Christian people will be filled with enduring love for God and the gospel of our salvation. We pray:

For the priests, deacons, and ministers of the church, that the Spirit will bring to fulfillment the good work begun in them. We pray:

For the gift of gratitude, that everywhere God's faithful people will offer a joyful sacrifice of praise in union with Christ. We pray:

For those who labor to build a house for the church, that their work and artistry may bring greater glory to God. We pray:

For the church that gathers in humble surroundings, may these faith communities enjoy the rich gifts of the Spirit. We pray:

For all the faithful departed, that they may be found praising God in the heavenly temple. We pray:

Presider: God in heaven, hear our prayers and sustain your church in the power of your Holy Spirit. We ask this through Christ, our Lord.

St. Martin of Tours (November 11)

[November 11 is also Veterans Day in the U.S. and Remembrance Day in Canada.]

Presider: Professing our belief that Christ Jesus is God from God and Light from Light, let us pray for a strengthening of our catholic and apostolic faith.

Petition Leader: Our response is, **"Spirit of truth, be our light."**

We believe Christ is the eternal Word who became flesh. May the Catholic church hold fast to its faith in word and in deed. We pray:

We believe Christ Jesus was like us in all things but sin. May all the baptized strive to set aside all encumbrance of sin and pursue the way of Christ. We pray:

We believe Christ Jesus died and rose again. May we always embrace the gospel of life and work to eliminate hatred and violence among us. We pray:

We believe the Holy Spirit re-creates us in grace. May the church's ministry of word and sacrament sustain the faithful on their life's journey. We pray:

We believe in a new heaven and new earth. May Christ, who has been given full authority of the new creation, fill us with enduring peace and respect for life. We pray:

We believe in the communion of saints. May our friendship with all the holy ones help us to be instruments of God's compassionate love, as was St. Martin of Tours. We pray:

We believe in the resurrection of the dead. May all who have died, especially veterans who protected human rights and well-being, be raised to life through the mercy of God. We pray:

We believe our faith summons us to act justly. May we use our voices to advocate human rights, especially freedom to live in accord with one's faith. We pray:

Presider: God, your Word is Spirit and life. Hear our prayers, keep us united in faith, and by the prayers and example of St. Martin of Tours, may we live honorably and peaceably. Through Christ, our Lord.

St. Frances Xavier Cabrini (November 13)

Presider: As we honor the memory of St. Frances Cabrini, let us pray that all will have the heart and mind of Jesus Christ.

Petition Leader: Our prayer response is, **"Christ, our Life, hear us."**

Beloved of God, you were sent to bring good news to the poor and brokenhearted. May the missionary efforts of the church renew human hopes through the gospel's proclamation. We ask in faith:

Word of God, you call us to be refreshed in your love. May the church's ministry among the homeless and refugees be blessed by your Spirit. We ask in faith:

Savior of all, you call us, as you called St. Frances Cabrini, to care for the stranger in our midst. May we act as you commanded by extending hospitality to immigrants. We ask in faith:

Light of the world, you summon your church to be an enlightened city on a hilltop. May the light of your love burn brightly through our work to relieve human misery. We ask in faith:

Bread of Life, you fill the hungry with good things. May our parishes be havens of compassion sustained on your life-giving sacraments. We ask in faith:

Son of God, you are our reconciliation and peace. May your Spirit bring tranquillity to all who are in periods of depression and despair. We ask in faith:

[The following petition may be added where appropriate.]
Risen Savior, you animated the heart of St. Frances Cabrini with the fire of your love. Continue to claim for yourself and your church the lives of the Missionaries of the Sacred Heart. We ask in faith:

Presider: Christ Jesus, you bid us to ask that we may receive. Hear our prayers, and by the example and intercession of your holy servant, Frances Cabrini, may our own hearts be kindled with the fires of faith, hope, and love. We make our prayer in your name and Spirit.

St. Elizabeth of Hungary (November 17)

Presider: Let us be mindful of the poor and hungry among us that we may act with compassion as did St. Elizabeth of Hungary.

Petition Leader: Our response today is, **"Christ, our Living Bread, hear us."**

May we be empowered by your Spirit to be generous with our daily bread, that all may be fed. Believing you are the Bread of Life, we pray:

May we hasten to extend care to the sick, especially those who have no caregivers or family. Believing your love is healing, we pray:

May we be enlightened to any greed and racism in our hearts that we may be healed through your mercy. Believing that your grace transforms our lives, we pray:

May we be filled with hope when poverty, unemployment, and illness mark our days. Believing that your love sustains us in time of trial, we pray:

May we keep faith, as did St. Elizabeth, when death robs us of those we love, particularly our children. Believing you are the Resurrection and Life, we pray:

May we act with courage and patience when we are falsely accused as was St. Elizabeth. Believing that your passion and death have given us new life, we pray:

May we be found rich in the harvest of justice when our life is ended. Believing you will come to judge the living and dead, we pray:

Presider: Christ Jesus, you were sent to be our Living Bread. Hear us, we pray, and may our hearts, like St. Elizabeth's, be open to hear what you ask of us through your gospel and the cries of the poor, for you live and reign forever.

St. Rose Philippine Duchesne (November 18)

Presider: St. Rose Philippine Duchesne was filled with enduring love for God and neighbor. Assisted by her prayers, let us pray that our lives will be filled with the fire of love kindled from the heart of Christ.

Petition Leader: Our prayer response is, **"Holy Spirit, kindle in us the fire of your love."**

Mindful that God's love creates all things in heaven and on earth, may we live reverently and respectfully during our pilgrimage. Calling on Christ's Spirit, we ask:

Remembering that Christ commands us to love one another, may all the members of the body of Christ, the church, be free of hatred and enmity. Calling on Christ's Spirit, we ask:

Rejoicing that Christ has called us to share in his mission of mercy, may every Christian act with compassion at home and in public. Calling on Christ's Spirit, we ask:

Responding in faith to Christ's call in the Spirit, may all who have vowed their lives to God and service to the church be centers of persevering prayer as was St. Rose. Calling on Christ's Spirit, we ask:

Confident that God hears our prayer of faith, may all who seek God's healing and reconciliation in the sacraments of the church be filled with peace. Calling on Christ's Spirit, we ask:

Believing that in Christ there is neither Jew nor Greek, slave nor free, male nor female, may every Christian community strive for greater equality among its members. Calling on Christ's Spirit, we ask:

Presider: God in heaven, may the fire of love burn brightly in our lives that we may shine with the glory of Christ in the resurrection of the just. Grant this in Jesus' name.

St. Andrew Dung-Lac and Martyrs of Vietnam (November 24)

Presider: Remembering that Christ calls us to take up our cross and follow in his footsteps, let us pray to be faithful disciples of a Crucified Redeemer.

Petition Leader: Our response today is, **"Christ, our Peace, hear us."**

For the Catholic church in Vietnam, may its bishops together with the faithful of Christ be a healing presence and a vibrant community of faith. We pray:

For Vietnamese who have left their homeland to build new lives, may they find in their adopted countries kind welcome and supportive friends. We pray:

For the Vietnamese people who carry within them the scars of war and death, may God's anointing Spirit guide them to full recovery. We pray:

For military and civilian personnel who continue to suffer the effects of war, may they find in Christ, the Healer, restored health and tranquillity. We pray:

For persecuted Christians, may the example and courageous faith of the Vietnamese martyrs be an inspiration in time of trial and hardship. We pray:

For Christians who persecute others, may all ill-will and malice in the followers of Jesus be dispelled by the light of God's Spirit. We pray:

For all the dead, especially innocent victims of war, may the merciful Christ bid the company of martyrs to lead them into paradise. We pray:

Presider: God of perfect peace, hear our prayers and receive the intercession of St. Andrew and companions on our behalf. May we strive to be instruments of Christ's peace and come to its fullness in the reign of heaven. Grant this in Jesus' name.

St. Francis Xavier (December 3)

Presider: Let us pray that all the world may come to know Christ, whom St. Francis Xavier proclaimed.

Petition Leader: Our response today is, **"Light of Nations, hear us!"**

Through the proclamation of the gospel and the church's work of evangelization, may every culture be imbued with the Spirit of Christ for the world's salvation. As we await the Dawn of Justice, we pray:

Through the intercession of St. Francis Xavier, may the Catholic church throughout Asia and the Pacific offer vibrant witness to Christ. As we await the Dawn of Justice, we pray:

Through the sacraments of new life, may each local church be built up into Christian communities rich in faith and love for Christ. As we await the Dawn of Justice, we pray:

Through the working of the Holy Spirit, may many women and men be inspired to dedicate their lives as missionaries. As we await the Dawn of Justice, we pray:

Through the church's work on behalf of God's reign, may the plight of the economically poor, the sick, and the uneducated be alleviated. As we await the Dawn of Justice, we pray:

Presider: God, you have given us Christ to be our Light. Hear our prayers and may your church kindle in the hearts of all peoples the light of faith that the world may be vigilant in hope. Grant this through Christ, our Lord.

Bl. Juan Diego (December 9)

May the prayers of Juan Diego, in union with Mary, secure for the peoples of the Americas every spiritual blessing that Christ may be all in all. We pray:

[Also see "Any Saint or Blessed," pages 170-171.]

Our Lady of Guadalupe (December 12)

Presider: God, the Creator of the human family, has called us to a holy way of life. On this feast of Mary, Patroness of the Americas, let us pray to be faithful to the Spirit of her Son.

Petition Leader: Our response today is, **"God, fill us with your grace."**

Let us pray for the Spirit of good counsel, who overshadowed Mary, that the church may proclaim with tender love the word of life. We humbly ask:

Let us pray for the Spirit of wisdom, that the church united in love with Mary will lay before the world the richness of the gospel of the poor. We humbly ask:

Let us pray for the Spirit of love, that God may dwell in us through grace and make us one with Mary, the ark of the new covenant. We humbly ask:

Let us pray for the Spirit of unity, that all nations and races may live in peace under the prayerful protection of the Mother of God. We humbly ask:

Let us pray for the Spirit of compassion, that our hearts may remain open to the cries of the oppressed as Mary's heart is an open refuge and sanctuary of Christ's mercy. We humbly ask:

Let us pray for the Spirit of light, that the peoples of the Americas, strengthened by Mary's intercession, may advance in their respect for life. We humbly ask:

Presider: Gracious God, hear the prayers of your church united in the one Spirit with the Mother of the Redeemer. May we enjoy your favor and know your blessings through Christ, our Lord.

St. John of the Cross (December 14)

Presider: On this feast of St. John of the Cross let us call upon Christ, the Radiant Dawn, to fill us with joyful hope.

Petition Leader: Our response today is, **"Christ, fill us with hope."**

For the church as it contemplates the mystery of Christ, may the dying and rising of Jesus continue to be our source of hope and joy. As we await the coming of Christ, we ask:

For persons burdened by guilt for past sins, may the cross of Christ and the promise of a new heaven and earth bring peace of heart and mind. As we await the coming of Christ, we ask:

For all who are in periods of spiritual darkness and suffering, may they not grow weary in their desire for union with Christ, the Light of Life. As we await the coming of Christ, we ask:

For the grace of conversion for all whose hopes and joys are centered in themselves and the perishable things of this creation. As we await the coming of Christ, we ask:

For the gift of patience and trust in conflict situations, may the example and prayers of John of the Cross help us to place our hope in God's power to heal and save. As we await the coming of Christ, we ask:

[The following petition may be added where appropriate.]
For the Carmelite communities throughout the world, may they be blessed with the gifts of wisdom and love as they celebrate the victory of Christ on this feast of John of the Cross. As we await the coming of Christ, we ask:

For the gift of love by which we arrive at the City of Joy, may we labor to remove from our hearts and minds all obstacles that would keep us from rejoicing with the saints in light. As we await the coming of Christ, we ask:

Presider: God in heaven, fill us with the light of faith and sustain us in joyful hope. May our prayers be acceptable to you and our lives pleasing in your sight, as was the life of your servant, John. Grant this through Christ, our Hope of Glory.

Holy Innocents (December 28)

Presider: Christ came among us as the world's Salvation. Let us call upon the Savior to bless us, especially children, with peace and good health.

Petition Leader: Our response is, **"Lord of life, hear us."**

Protect us from all harm and safeguard the well-being of our children, we pray:

Surround children with good teachers and witnesses of your abiding care, we pray:

Help parents to be faithful examples of your love and tenderness in the lives of the young, we pray:

Bless abundantly health-care programs and services that serve infants and children, we pray:

Console by your Spirit parents who grieve the loss of a child, we pray: Embrace with your eternal love all infants and children who have died from neglect and violence, we pray:

Inspire nations to safeguard the rights of all people and free our world from crimes of hate, we pray:

Receive into the enduring peace of heaven all who died giving witness to Christ, we pray:

Presider: God of glory, your love is manifest in our midst in Christ, the Prince of Peace. In the name of your beloved Son, we ask you to keep us safe and free from all harm. Grant this through Christ, our Light.

Mass of the Blessed Virgin Mary in Advent

[The following is suitable for use with any of the Mass formularies for the BVM in Advent.]

Presider: Believing as did Mary in the promise of salvation, let us pray that the church will grow stronger in faith, hope, and love.

Petition Leader: Our response is, **"Saving God, hear our prayer."**

For the church united with Mary in the mystery of Christ, may it continually hasten with the gospel of peace into the hill country of human need. We pray in joyful hope:

For all the baptized, may the lives of the faithful bear the fruit of salvation through the grace of the Holy Spirit who overshadowed the Mother of Jesus. We pray in joyful hope:

For all catechumens as they prepare for baptism, may they consent in faith to God's saving will as did Mary of Nazareth. We pray in joyful hope:

For all who place their lives in loving service of God and neighbor, may their dedication remain constant through the help of Mary's intercession. We pray in joyful hope:

For all the dead who trusted in God's word of redemption, may they be joined to Mary in her everlasting canticle of praise. We pray in joyful hope:

Presider: O God, you have favored us with your love and grace. Receive our prayers and keep your church rooted in Christ, the Word of Life, whom Mary bore in her womb. We ask this through Christ, the Promise of Ages who lives forever.

Mass of the Blessed Virgin Mary in Lent

[The following is suitable for use with any of the Mass formularies for the BVM in Lent or for the memorial of Our Lady of Sorrows, September 15.]

Presider: Mary stood in solidarity with her Son in his suffering. Let us call upon the Spirit of Jesus to make us strong disciples of a crucified Messiah.

Petition Leader: Our response today is, **"Giver of Life, hear us."**

Mary gave courageous witness at the foot of the cross. May the church provide the world with a strong witness to the gospel of reconciliation. We pray:

Mary became a partner with Christ in his passion. May we unite ourselves daily to the sacrifice of Christ and become more fully a priestly people. We pray:

Mary stood firm in adversity with her crucified Son who brought forth new life. Through her prayers and the Spirit's power may we nurture new life for victims of violence and poverty. We pray:

[Omit the following petition for the memorial of Our Lady of Sorrows.]
The death of Jesus brought unity and healing to a divided world. May our Lenten journey to Calvary empower us to foster nonviolent solutions to conflicts. We pray:

Most of the disciples fled the scene of crucifixion. May the Spirit of God and Mary's enduring love help us to extend the mercy of Christ to any who suffer. We pray:

Christ gave his life to ransom sinners from death. Through Mary's intercession and our encouragement may many be reconciled to God. We pray:

Christ commended his mother to the beloved disciple. May Mary, the faithful disciple, commend us to Christ when the hour of death is upon us. We pray:

Presider: Redeeming God, you have reconciled us to yourself in Christ. May we who call upon your Spirit of new life be strengthened in faith, hope, and love, especially in time of trial. Grant our prayers through Christ, our Peacemaker with you forever.

Mass of the Blessed Virgin Mary in the Easter Season

[The following is suitable with any of the Mass formularies for the BVM in the Easter season.]

Presider: Let us pray in the spirit of Easter joy.

Petition Leader: Our prayer response today is, "Risen Savior, hear our prayer."

Christ, the Sun of Justice, has destroyed the darkness of death. May all the newly baptized, who have been given the light of Christ, unite in Mary's praise of God. With renewed hearts, we pray:

The resurrection brings joy to the homes of all believers. May the church, the dwelling place of Christ in the Spirit, resound with joy at the table of life. With renewed hearts, we pray:

Inspired by Mary's vigilant prayer for the promised Holy Spirit, may we use our spiritual gifts to foster harmony in our homes and world. With renewed hearts, we pray:

The Spirit, who raised Jesus from the dead, has been poured into our hearts. May we, as does Mary, show ourselves to be sanctuaries of new life. With renewed hearts, we pray:

Clothed in the glory of her risen Son, Mary shines forth as our hope. May all the dead, who longed to be bathed in eternal light, be helped by her prayers. With renewed hearts, we pray:

Presider: God of matchless glory, you have shown us the greatness of your love in raising Jesus from the dead. Receive the prayers of your church and the intercession of Mary as we praise you through Christ, our risen Savior.

Mass of the Blessed Virgin Mary in Ordinary Time
Option #1

[The following intercessions may also be used "For the Spread of the Gospel."]

Presider: Through intercessory prayer we call upon the Holy Spirit to lead us to the glory of God.

Petition Leader: Our response today is, **"May all praise your glory, O God!"**

That all whose faith is nurtured on the Hebrew and Christian scriptures will find in the word of God the inspiration to build strong communities of faith, we pray:

That missionaries will find the Creator's image and the Spirit's gifts of faith, hope, and love awaiting them in the people they serve, we pray:

That catechists and pastoral ministers will be strengthened by God's grace as they strive to nurture in youth a personal love for God, we pray:

That those who spread the gospel through the arts will increasingly cherish their gifts as an indispensable witness to the Creator's beauty and truth, we pray:

That all who are discerning the Spirit's voice to work on behalf of the gospel will be supported by the intercession of Mary, the Mother of Jesus, we pray:

That our celebration of the eucharist will draw us closer to the Spirit and intensify our longing for a life of endless praise of God's glory, we pray:

Presider: God, Source of all life and truth, you have given us the Word of everlasting life in Christ, your Son. Receive our prayers and bring us to the glory of risen life in the company of Mary and all the saints. In Jesus' name we pray.

Mass of the Blessed Virgin Mary in Ordinary Time
Option #2

[The following intercessions are suitable for use when celebrating a Mass that honors Mary as the Mother of Mercy, Health of the Sick, Help of Christians, or Queen of Peace.]

Presider: Fortified by the gospel of Jesus Christ, we pray.

Petition Leader: Today, in union with Mary, let us be confident in our prayer as we call upon the Savior of all humankind and say, **"Let new life flow within us, O Christ!"**

That the world's spiritual and political leaders will be open to the Spirit's inspirations to seek universal peace by encouraging nonviolence in daily living, we pray:

That all who witness to the gospel through a ministry of prayer will find blessing as they call down the Spirit upon our church and world, we pray:

That persons in periods of recovery from major illness, addictions, or abuse may be renewed in spirit through personal prayer and the sacraments of healing, we pray:

That the church, united with Mary in prayer, will not hesitate to present to Christ the pressing needs of others that are brought to our attention, we pray:

That we will be strengthened by Mary's intercession to break every form of captivity that oppresses human life, especially sin, we pray:

That the blessings we receive through the eucharist will enable us to emulate Mary's compassion by being attentive to the cries of the poor, we pray:

That Mary will bear within her heart the personal needs and concerns we place before Christ this day [pause for silent prayer], we pray:

Presider: God, our Creator and Savior, you desire that all peoples praise your glory. See in our prayers our desire to fulfill your will in all times and places. Through Mary's prayer sustain us by your Word and Spirit. We ask this through Christ, our Lord.

Mass of the Blessed Virgin Mary in Ordinary Time
Option #3

[These petitions draw on themes found in the collection of Masses of the BVM in ordinary time.]

Presider: As a priestly people in union with Mary let us call upon Christ, the fountain of new life.

Petition Leader: Our response today is, **"Lord, give us living water!"**

For all who thirst for the compassion of God. May the church, united in Spirit to the Mother of Mercy, embrace the broken-hearted and the sinner with the love of Christ. We pray:

For peoples who thirst for freedom. May the followers of Christ, together with the Mother of Ransom, work to undue the bondage of oppression. We pray:

For any who thirst for renewed strength as they minister to the sick and dying. May we, encouraged by Mary's attentive love, be supportive of care-givers. We pray:

For persons who thirst for spiritual truths. May our prayers, and Mary's contemplation of God's love, call forth the Spirit's gifts for all spiritual seekers. We pray:

For any who thirst for healthier environments. May our respect for God's creation deepen while we wait with Mary for the new heaven and earth. We pray:

For all who thirst for healing as they journey to sacred sites, especially those bearing Mary's name. May all pilgrims be blessed with peace and reconciliation. We pray:

For all who thirst for the words of everlasting life. May our prayers, united to Mary's unceasing praise, assist those who have died hoping in Christ. We pray:

Presider: God, Healer and Sustainer of souls, you refresh us from the fountain of life, who is Christ born of Mary. Hear our prayers made in the power of Jesus' name.

Immaculate Heart of Mary

Presider: Let us pray with hearts that are centered in God.

Petition Leader: Our response is, **"Come, Spirit of God, bless us!"**

May the Holy Spirit fashion our hearts so that they may receive the Word of Life in faith and contemplate its truth. With Mary we rejoice in God's love and ask:

May the Holy Spirit free our hearts from sin so that we may more clearly see God in the daily events of our lives. With Mary we rejoice in God's love and ask:

May the Holy Spirit fill our hearts with enduring compassion for all who suffer and are victims of injustice. With Mary we rejoice in God's love and ask:

May the Holy Spirit sanctify our hearts so that we may pursue integrity of word and deed in our lives. With Mary we rejoice in God's love and ask:

May the Holy Spirit keep our hearts watchful in prayer that the church may treasure God's abundant blessings. With Mary we rejoice in God's love and ask:

May the Holy Spirit instill wisdom in our hearts that we may remain obedient to the gospel of eternal life. With Mary we rejoice in God's love and ask:

Presider: Gracious God, fill us with your Spirit, the Divine Teacher, who leads us to the truth of your redeeming love, through Christ, our Savior.

Any Apostle
Option #1

Presider: Let us pray in the spirit of faith that marked the lives of the apostles.

Petition Leader: Our response is: **"God, hear our prayer."**

For the church; in union with Mary, the first among apostles, may all who profess faith in the apostolic mission of the church set out in haste with the gospel of peace. We ask:

For each local church; may the faithful with their bishop be a vibrant community of faith united to the Bishop of Rome. We ask:

For all who undertake the works of mercy; may the intercession of St.(s) [Name(s)] be a source of encouragement for all who minister to persons in need. We ask:

For our parish family; may the faith community of [Name of parish] be united in one spirit and offer warm welcome to friends and strangers. We ask:

For the spread of the gospel; may we encourage lay and religious vocations to the foreign missions that all may hear the Word of Life. We ask:

For ourselves; may we continually use our voices to proclaim gospel values in both public and private life. We ask:

For the dead (especially _____); may all who professed their faith in the resurrection of Christ rejoice in the company of St.(s) [Name(s)]. We ask:

Presider: Loving God, through the teaching and preaching mission of your servant church, your gospel reaches the ends of the earth. In your mercy hear our prayers. Enliven our faith through the Spirit of Christ whom you poured into the hearts of the apostles. Grant this in Jesus' name.

Any Apostle
Option #2

Presider: Rejoicing in the word of salvation, let us pray that its message reaches the ends of the earth.

Petition Leader: Our response is, **"Word of Life, receive our prayer."**

Christ Jesus is the good news of God's compassionate love. May the church live the gospel of compassion and celebrate its hope. We pray:

Christ, the Revealer of God's love, has called us to share in his saving mission. May all the baptized witness to Christ by holiness of life. We pray:

Christ gathered the apostles and disciples to himself that the harvest of justice would have many workers. Through the intercession of St. [*Name*] may many men and women respond to Christ's call. We pray:

Christ entrusted the apostles with proclaiming the gospel to all nations. May the apostolic ministry of Pope [*Name*] and the church's bishops be received respectfully by all the faithful. We pray:

Christ sent Mary Magdalene as an apostle to the apostles with the joyful news of the resurrection. May the church joyfully receive the apostolic gifts the Spirit bestows among all the members of Christ. We pray:

Christ assured the apostles that the Spirit would lead them to all truth. May the Spirit lead all the dead to the reign of light where the apostles rejoice forever. We pray:

Presider: God of all creation, in Christ you have fixed a firm cornerstone upon which the church is built. May the gospel we have received through the preaching of St. [*Name*] root us firmly in Christ, the One whom you sent as the world's Redeemer, who lives forever.

Any Evangelist
Option #1

Presider: Today let us pray that the word of God will be the foundation of our life in Christ.

Petition Leader: Our response is: **"Lord, hear our prayer."**

That all Christians will grow in their knowledge and love for the sacred scriptures, we pray:

That our striving for spiritual maturity will draw us to deeper meditation on the gospels, we pray:

That the word of God will light our way to greater world peace, we pray:

That the ministry of scripture scholars and theologians will nourish God's people with greater insight on the mysteries of faith, we pray:

That proclaimers of the word and homilists will be blessed in their service to the church, we pray:

That the Spirit of truth, through the prayers of St. [*Name*], will lead us to greater intimacy with Christ, the Word-Made-Flesh, we pray:

Presider: Creating God, through your living Word we come to know the love you have for us. Hear our prayers, and may our love for sacred scripture draw us closer to you. We ask this in the name of your Word of Redemption, Jesus Christ.

Any Evangelist
Option #2

Presider: Fortified by God's word, let us pray that it will find a secure dwelling place in our hearts through faith.

Petition Leader: Our response today is, **"God, graciously hear us."**

May the Christian faithful always cherish the sacred writings of scripture and grow in their knowledge of and love for God. We pray:

May our contemplation of the mystery of Christ proclaimed by the gospel of St. [Name] help us to mature spiritually. We pray:

May the ministry of scripture scholars be guided by the Spirit that all may come to a deeper understanding of God's redeeming love. We pray:

May Christian spiritual writers use their gifts to serve God for the good of all who seek to know Christ, the Fountain of new life. We pray:

May the church's mission of evangelization flourish in the Spirit through the intercession of St. [Name]. We pray:

May we celebrate our blessedness in the company of St. [Name] for having heard the word of God and kept it all our days. We pray:

Presider: God in heaven, through your Word you have created all things. By that same saving Word you offer us life to the full. May we receive your gifts with open hearts. We ask this in Jesus' name.

Any Martyr

Presider: As we celebrate the life and death of St. [*Name*], let us be mindful of Christ's abiding care even in the face of death.

Petition Leader: Our response today is, **"Christ, Victor, hear our prayer."**

Death no longer has any power over Christ. May St. [*Name*], who was joined to Christ in life and death, intercede for all who are joined to Christ through baptism. Trusting in God's love, we pray:

Christ mediates for the church at the right hand of the Power. May St. [*Name*], who shares in Christ's heavenly ministry, inspire us to be a people of vigilant prayer. Trusting in God's love, we pray:

Christ promised that the Spirit would be with us always. May the strengthening Spirit uphold all who suffer for their witness to Christ. Trusting in God's love, we pray:

Christ taught that peacemakers would be known as God's daughters and sons. May all who aspire to be God's children eternally break with all violence to human life and dignity. Trusting in God's love, we pray:

Christ crucified has assumed every person's suffering that healing may come to all. May we be instruments of God's healing to all who suffer mental and emotional martyrdom. Trusting in God's love, we pray:

Christ promised to give refreshment to all who are heavily burdened. May all who have been burdened with death experience the liberating love of a crucified Redeemer (especially _____). Trusting in God's love, we pray:

Presider: Loving God, the power of your love has triumphed over sin and death. May the intercession of St. [*Name*] bring the sustaining Spirit of Christ to rest upon your pilgrim church. Grant our prayers in the name of Jesus, the First-born of the dead.

Martyrs (More Than One Martyr)

Presider: As we celebrate the life and death of Sts. [*Names*], let us be mindful of Christ's abiding care even in the face of death.

Petition Leader: Our response today is, **"Christ, Victor, hear our prayer."**

Death no longer has any power over Christ. May Sts. [*Names*], who were joined to Christ in life and death, intercede for all who are joined to Christ through baptism. Trusting in God's love, we pray:

Christ mediates for the church at the right hand of the Power. May Sts. [*Names*], who share in Christ's heavenly ministry, inspire us to be a people of vigilant prayer. Trusting in God's love, we pray:

Christ promised that the Spirit would be with us always. May the strengthening Spirit uphold all who suffer for their witness to Christ. Trusting in God's love, we pray:

Christ taught that peacemakers would be known as God's daughters and sons. May all who aspire to be God's children eternally break with all violence to human life and dignity. Trusting in God's love, we pray:

Christ crucified has assumed every person's suffering that healing may come to all. May we be instruments of God's healing to all who suffer mental and emotional martyrdom. Trusting in God's love, we pray:

Christ promised to give refreshment to all who are heavily burdened. May all who have been burdened with death experience the liberating love of a crucified Redeemer (especially _____). Trusting in God's love, we pray:

Presider: Loving God, the power of your love has triumphed over sin and death. May the intercession of Sts. [*Names*] bring the sustaining Spirit of Christ to rest upon your pilgrim church. Grant our prayers in the name of Jesus, the First-born of the dead.

Any Martyr (Woman)

Presider: In baptism we are called to die with Christ, so that sharing a likeness to his death we may share a like resurrection. On this memorial of St.(s) [*Name(s)*], let us pray for all who are victims of violence or suffer persecution for their religious and moral beliefs.

Petition Leader: Our response to each petition is: **"Renew our strength, God of mercy."**

For women whose lives are emotionally and psychologically destroyed by physical abuse and rape. Uniting with all the saintly women martyrs, we call out to God:

For families that are devastated by crimes of violence. Uniting with all the saintly women martyrs, we call out to God:

For men and women whose hearts have turned cold by aggressive military training. Uniting with all the saintly women martyrs, we call out to God:

For children who are victims of adult abuse. Uniting with all the saintly women martyrs, we call out to God:

For persons of all ages who are terrorized by unjust governments. Uniting with all the saintly women martyrs, we call out to God:

For individuals who are penalized for their solidarity with any who suffer unjustly, especially prisoners of conscience. Uniting with all the saintly women martyrs, we call out to God:

For persons who are victims of extortionists, especially the elderly. Uniting with all the saintly women martyrs, we call out to God:

For Christians who undergo physical and psychological torture for their faith commitment. Uniting with all the saintly women martyrs, we call out to God:

Presider: God of mercy, we are struck down but never destroyed, for your Spirit comes to help us in our weakness. Receive our prayers in union with the holy martyr(s) [*Name(s)*] in the name of Christ, our Redeemer.

Any Doctor of the Church

Presider: Let us invoke the Spirit, who animated St. [*Name*] with a love for God.

Petition Leader: Our response today is, **"Spirit of God, fill us with light."**

Come, Holy Spirit, fill Pope [*Name*] and the church's bishops with your grace that they may wisely proclaim the truth which sets us free in Christ. We pray:

Come, Spirit of knowledge, lavish upon Christian theologians a love for God that their teaching ministry may nourish the faithful. We pray:

Come, Spirit of wisdom, bestow upon all spiritual writers your gift of understanding holy mysteries for the spiritual good of God's people. We pray:

Come, Spirit of counsel, assist Christian believers that our actions may sincerely conform to the faith that St. [*Name*] lived well. We pray:

Come, Spirit of Jesus, teach us to pray that our hearts may contemplate the goodness of God. We pray:

Come, Spirit of fortitude, empower the Catholic community to be strong in its love in time of trial and disagreement. We pray:

Come, Spirit of life, raise up the dead who trusted in God's gracious mercy (especially _____). We pray:

Presider: God in heaven, hear our prayers and fill us with the Spirit of love who teaches us the deep mysteries of Christ. May we always cherish the faith that gave St. [*Name*] new life in Christ. We ask this in the name of Jesus.

Any Saint or Blessed
Option #1

Presider: Saint/Blessed [*Name*] lived by the light of faith in God's redeeming love. Let us pray that the Holy Spirit will continue to draw all people to God through the light of Christ.

Petition Leader: Our prayer response today is, **"Compassionate God, receive our prayer."**

May the Holy Spirit fill the hearts of all the followers of Christ with a deep love for God's word, that it may be the foundation of our life of faith. We pray:

May the sanctifying Spirit who filled Saint/Blessed [*Name*] with love for God and God's people continue to draw all nations into the peace of Christ. We pray:

[Another intercession for the saint or blessed whose feast or memorial is being celebrated may be included here.]

May the love of Christ we celebrate in this eucharist reveal itself in our readiness to be of service to those in need. We pray:

May the strengthening Spirit who heals us in Christ be with the sick, especially those who are terminally ill. We pray:

May the Spirit of wisdom who filled Saint/Blessed [*Name*] enrich the lives of all who search for God and fullness of life. We pray:

May the Spirit, who raised Jesus from the dead, bring all the dead to new life (especially _____). We pray:

Presider: Saving God, in your loving kindness, hear our prayers and uphold us in your grace. We pray in the name of Christ, our Redeemer.

Any Saint or Blessed
Option #2

[These are suitable for a saint or blessed noted for his or her apostolic works of mercy and justice.]

Presider: Let us pray for the needs of the church and the world in the spirit of faith that filled Saint/Blessed [*Name*].

Petition Leader: Our response today is, **"Christ Jesus, hear our prayer."**

May the Catholic church, together with Pope [*Name*] and all the bishops, continuously draw strength from the gospel of God's compassion. We ask in faith:

May the reconciling love of Christ that inspired Saint/Blessed [*Name*] to a life of compassionate service also fill us who feast at this holy table. We ask in faith:

[Another intercession for the saint or blessed whose feast or memorial is being celebrated may be included here.]

May all who long for peace in the world, in their homes or heart, be strengthened by the Holy Spirit and intercession of the saints. We ask in faith:

May the economically poor find in the Christian faithful strong advocates for justice and servants of God's love. We ask in faith:

May our sisters and brothers whose days are marked by illness know the healing love of Christ and the Spirit's consolation. We ask in faith:

May our beloved dead, who longed to share in the joy of the saints, be received with mercy by the risen Christ (especially _____). We ask in faith:

Presider: God of steadfast compassion, we rejoice in Christ who has saved us. Fill us with your grace, strengthen us by the intercession of the saints, and bring us to the fullness of life, through our Savior, Jesus Christ.

Special Circumstances

For Families
Option #1

Presider: Let us invoke God's kindness that families may live in harmony and mutual care.

Petition Leader: Our prayer response today is, **"God, fill us with your love."**

In you, O God, all life is birthed with love. Pour out the Spirit, the Giver of Life, upon the church, your family in Christ. We look to your kindness and ask:

In you, O God, all life is redeemed by love. Send forth the Spirit of truth to guide all families by the light of your Word. We look to your kindness and ask:

In you, O God, all life is sustained in love. Lavish your Spirit of wisdom upon each household that all may dwell secure. We look to your kindness and ask:

In you, O God, all life is enriched through love. Bestow the Spirit of grace upon spouses for their own good and the good of others. We look to your kindness and ask:

In you, O God, all life is protected by love. Safeguard by your Spirit the life of infants, children, and the elderly. We look to your kindness and ask:

In you, O God, all life is healed with love. Renew by your Spirit of unity families divided by anger and disregard. We look to your kindness and ask:

In you, O God, all life is embraced with love. Send forth your Spirit of hope to support families in periods of trial and hardship. We look to your kindness and ask:

In you, O God, all life is received with love. Raise up by your Spirit our loved ones who have died. We look to your kindness and ask:

Presider: God of loving kindness, hear our prayers of faith and trust offered to you in the name and Spirit of Jesus.

For Families
Option #2

Presider: Let us pray for God's strengthening gifts.

Petition Leader: Our response is, **"God, graciously hear us."**

For our families, that each member may be blessed with good health and peace of mind. Remembering God's love for us, we pray:

For single parents with dependent children, that they be blessed with caring relatives and strong community support. Remembering God's love for us, we pray:

For families of missing persons, that they may draw strength from the cross of Christ and experience Mary's consoling intercession. Remembering God's love for us, we pray:

For families torn apart by dissension, divorce, or addictions, that God's healing Spirit will restore tranquillity and new life. Remembering God's love for us, we pray:

For immigrant and refugee families working to make a new home among us, that they will find rich hospitality and welcome in our parishes. Remembering God's love for us, we pray:

For families faced with economic hardship, that the care and concern of others will come to their aid, especially through helpful legislation. Remembering God's love for us, we pray:

For families grieving the loss of a loved one, that their faith in Christ's resurrection will bring comfort and hope. Remembering God's love for us, we pray:

Presider: God, your love has brought us to life and your Spirit gathers us to be a new family in Christ. Hear our prayers for all families. May your grace keep us united in love as we journey to the kingdom. Grant this through Christ, the First-born of many sisters and brothers.

For Vocation Discernment

[The following petitions may be used in whole or part where it is appropriate to pray for vocations.]

Presider: Mindful that the church is called to serve Christ, let us pray that the Spirit of the Lord will enrich the community of believers with vocations.

Petition Leader: Our response today is, **"Come, Holy Spirit!"**

For the gift of discernment, that the Spirit of God will guide the church at prayer and those who seek to know God's will in their lives. Relying on God's help, we pray:

For the gift of fidelity, that the Spirit of love may enable us to have the heart and mind of Christ, who came to minister to others. Relying on God's help, we pray:

For the gift of right judgment, that the Spirit of counsel will guide individuals pondering a vocation and those who serve as their spiritual or vocation directors. Relying on God's help, we pray:

For the gift of generosity, that the Spirit, who dispenses every blessing, will inspire others to commit their lives totally in service to God and the church. Relying on God's help, we pray:

For the gift of peace, that the consoling Spirit may help those considering a vocation to overcome any fear and anxiety. Relying on God's help, we pray:

For the gift of personal prayer, that the Spirit of holiness may draw us into the intimacy of the Trinity and speak to our hearts. Relying on God's help, we pray:

For the gift of obedience to God's will, that the begetting Spirit may fulfill in us through grace, and the intercession of Mary, the mystery of Christ. Relying on God's help, we pray:

Presider: Redeeming God, we rely on your grace to guide us in all our ways. Strengthen in love those who call upon you, and enlighten those who are discerning a vocation. May our hearts be ever open to hear what you ask of us in the Spirit, through Christ, our Savior.

For Religious
Option #1

[The following petitions may be used in whole or part where it is appropriate to pray for religious.]

Presider: Let us pray on behalf of the women and men religious who have consecrated their lives to Christ and service to God's people.

Petition Leader: Our response today is, **"God, send forth your Spirit."**

We rejoice in God's invitation to have the fullness of life in Christ. May the church's religious exemplify the joy of loving God above all things. We pray:

We rejoice in God's call to share the intimacy of the Trinity. May the church's religious walk humbly with God and be blessed with peace. We pray:

We rejoice in God, our Savior, who reconciles everything through Christ. May the church's religious herald the new creation in word and deed. We pray:

We rejoice in God's merciful love that welcomes the sinner. May the church's religious be instruments of God's compassionate love in the lives of others. We pray:

We rejoice in God's liberating love that frees the world from death. May the church's religious vigorously pursue justice for the life of the world. We pray:

We rejoice in God's wisdom that invites all to feast at the table. May the church's religious find spiritual nourishment in God's word. We pray:

We rejoice in God's favor that lifts the lowly to high places. May the church's religious, fortified by Mary's intercession, set their hearts on the reign of heaven. We pray:

Presider: God of love and Abba of Jesus, hear us invoking your Spirit for the church's religious. By your Spirit bring to completion the good you have begun in them. Grant this in Jesus' name.

For Religious
Option #2

[For apostolic religious whose charism is compassionate service. It is suggested that these petitions be led by a religious.]

Presider: Let us summon the Spirit, who inspires us to serve God and God's people.

Petition Leader: Our response is, **"Dwell among us, O Spirit of God!"**

As we strive to provide safe havens for those in need, may God bless abundantly the many residences and shelters staffed by religious. We pray:

As we work with persons in their struggle to build a new life, may God's grace sustain the health-care and social service ministries sponsored by the church's religious communities. We pray:

As we undertake ministries of education that cultivate human and spiritual flourishing, may the Spirit guide Catholic academic institutions and programs. We pray:

As we address critical issues of universal human rights and dignity of persons, may the Spirit strengthen us for the works of peace and justice. We pray:

As we struggle to balance lives of active service and personal prayer, may the Spirit keep kindled in us the fires of love for God. We pray:

As we confront the counterforces to God's love in ourselves, our religious communities, our church, and the world, may the Spirit inspire our continuous conversion and lead us more deeply into the Paschal mystery. We pray:

Presider: God, rich in mercy, pour out your Spirit upon your daughters and sons who have consecrated themselves totally to Christ as religious. May their lives continue to enflesh anew your steadfast love, especially for those most in need. Grant our prayer in Jesus' name.

For Religious
Option #3

[For apostolic religious. It is suggested that these petitions be led by a religious.]

Presider: Let us pray.

Petition Leader: Our response is, **"God, receive our prayer."**

For those called to roles of leadership; may these sisters/brothers serve the needs of all thereby fulfilling the teaching of Christ. Trusting in God's love, we ask:

For any who are considering a vocation to religious life; may the Holy Spirit guide many new vocations to our community/communities. Trusting in God's love, we ask:

For our sisters/brothers serving in mission countries; may they be strengthened in their commitment to proclaim God's compassion to all peoples. Trusting in God's love, we ask:

For those who are struggling in their commitment to religious life; may their struggle be a holy one leading to deeper union with Christ and God's people. Trusting in God's love, we ask:

For our sisters/brothers who feel overwhelmed by the immensity of human misery; may the Spirit help them to overcome any discouragement as we strive to relieve suffering. Trusting in God's love, we ask:

For our sisters/brothers who are retired, elderly, and ill; may the Holy Spirit give them every grace in keeping with the riches of Christ. Trusting in God's love, we ask:

For our deceased sisters/brothers; may the Spirit, who raised Jesus from the dead, fill them with everlasting joy (especially _____). Trusting in God's love, we ask:

Presider: God, Source of Life and Light, receive our prayers. Uphold your servants in love and bring to completion the good you have begun in us/them through Christ, our risen brother and Redeemer.

For Religious
Option #4

[For monastic or contemplative religious. It is also suitable for all religious who profess the evangelical counsels. It is suggested that the petitions be led by a religious.]

Presider: Let us summon the Spirit of Christ, who brings all good things to perfection according to God's design.

Petition Leader: Our response is, **"Spirit of Christ, uphold us."**

May the Spirit, Lover of the poor, sanctify our poverty that we might grow rich in Christ. With trusting faith, we ask:

May the Paraclete, our Advocate, kindle in us the fire of holiness that our chaste love for God will imbue all our actions. With trusting faith, we ask:

May the Giver of Life beget in us the fidelity of Jesus that we may be obedient to God's redeeming will. With trusting faith, we ask:

[The following petition should be adapted accordingly.]
May the Spirit of unity keep us one in heart and mind with [Name], our [*abbot/abbess* or *prior/prioress*], that the peace of Christ may be our daily blessing. With trusting faith, we ask:

May the Spirit, the soul's delightful Guest, inspire our praise in union with the Mother of God. With trusting faith, we ask:

May the Spirit of light reveal the way to even deeper intimacy with the Word of Life. With trusting faith, we ask:

May the Spirit of love help us to contemplate the groaning of creation, and our own voice in it, through the eyes of a crucified Redeemer. With trusting faith, we ask:

Presider: God in heaven, may the Spirit who searches all hearts bring the weakness of our prayer to perfection in your sight. By grace may your servants grow more like Christ, the First-born of many brothers and sisters. Grant this in the name of Jesus.

For Priests

[Additional petitions have been included here to provide a rich selection. It is recommended that no more than five or six intercessions be used.]

Presider: Let us pray for those called to share in the ministerial priesthood of Jesus Christ.

Petition Leader: Our response is, **"Christ Jesus, hear our prayer."**

Rejoicing in God's redeeming love, may the Savior fortify priests in their commitment to serve God and God's people. We pray to the Lord:

Rejoicing in the word of salvation, may Christ give to all priests a deep love for the sacred scriptures. We pray to the Lord:

Rejoicing in the Holy Spirit, may the Lord continuously sanctify the lives of all priests that they may be holy as God is holy. We pray to the Lord:

Rejoicing in the Trinity, may all priests be blessed with a spirit of prayer and the gift of compassionate love for others. We pray to the Lord:

Rejoicing in God's healing love, may priests in periods of recovery from illness or addictions be blessed with renewed health. We pray to the Lord:

Rejoicing in unity of the Holy Spirit, may the priests of the church find in Mary consolation and hope. We pray to the Lord:

Rejoicing in Christ, the one Mediator of all, may the sacramental ministry of priests be fruitful in the Spirit for the salvation of God's people. We pray to the Lord:

Rejoicing in God our Savior, may priests be blessed with gifts that gather God's people together into vibrant communities of faith. We pray to the Lord:

Rejoicing in God's promise of eternal life, may deceased priests (especially _____) be received with mercy by Christ, the true and eternal Priest. We pray to the Lord:

Presider: Almighty God, we entrust to your care those whom you have called in the one Spirit to be priests. In your mercy forgive their sins and failings. Bring to completion the good you have begun in them for the honor and glory of your name. Hear our prayers through Christ, our Redeemer.

For Deacons and Ministers of the Church

Presider: Let us pray for the deacons of the church and all in roles of service for the good of God's people.

Petition Leader: Our response is, **"Christ Jesus, hear our prayer."**

For the Catholic church, Pope [*Name*], our bishop, [*Name*], and the church's clergy and ministers; may the servants in Christ's household enjoy the diverse gifts of the Holy Spirit. In faith we pray:

For the deacons of the church; may their ministry of word and service be blessed for the common good. In faith we pray:

For the wives and children of deacons; may their love for God and neighbor enrich the Christian community. In faith we pray:

For proclaimers of the word and catechists; may their service to God's people help deepen within the faithful the gospel of peace. In faith we pray:

For those who bring comfort to the sick, especially as ministers of the eucharist; may they encounter Christ in others as they share the Bread of Life. In faith we pray:

For pastoral musicians, choirs, and cantors; may those who help us to sing God's praises be filled with the Spirit's joy. In faith we pray:

For those who accompany the ill and lonely as spiritual caregivers; may they continue to be strengthened by God for the works of compassion. In faith we pray:

For those whose service to the church remains unseen; may God, who sees what no one else sees, bless and keep them. In faith we pray:

Presider: Loving God, how great is your name through all the earth! You bless your church abundantly with faithful servants. May we show our gratitude through our support and prayers which we make in Jesus' name.

For Christian Unity

Presider: Let us pray in the one Spirit for the Church's unity and peace.

Petition Leader: Our response is, **"Christ, our Life, bless and heal us."**

For all who have been baptized in Christ and profess the one Christian faith; may the Spirit of Unity draw Christian communions closer to each other. With joyful hope we pray:

For the leaders of the Christian churches; may their ministry help to deepen the bonds of respect among all followers of Christ. With joyful hope we pray:

For an increased commitment for dialogue among the churches; may the Holy Spirit keep kindled within Christians the spirit of ecumenism inspired by the Second Vatican Council. With joyful hope we pray:

For an end to hostility among the disciples of Jesus; may the Spirit purify our hearts and minds of any arrogance or anger that hinders Christian unity. With joyful hope we pray:

For families composed of different Christian traditions; may their example of harmonious and respectful living provide inspiration to all. With joyful hope we pray:

Presider: Loving God, Trinity of perfect unity, hear our prayers, and by your gifts of grace bring together into one household all Christian peoples, that your praises may be sung in one communion of love, through Christ, our Savior.

For the Spread of the Gospel
Option #1

Presider: Let our prayers call forth the strengthening Spirit of God for all who labor on behalf of the gospel.

Petition Leader: Our response is, **"Spirit of Jesus, abide with us."**

Christ Jesus, you came to proclaim the good news of God's love to the poor, sick, and broken-hearted. May the Catholic church be tireless in serving the gospel of compassion. Relying on your help, we pray:

Christ Jesus, you came anointed in the Spirit to be a light to the nations. May all who have committed their lives and time to spreading the light of your word be blessed abundantly. Relying on your help, we pray:

Christ Jesus, you formed a new person from Gentile and Jew. May your work of uniting all peoples into one communion of love continue through the ministry of each local church. Relying on your help, we pray:

Christ Jesus, you promised life-giving waters to all who come to you. May those who receive your Word of Life in faith be refreshed. Relying on your help, we pray:

Christ Jesus, you revealed yourself to be the Living Bread of God's love. May the sacramental ministry of your church sustain the faith of the baptized. Relying on your help, we pray:

Christ Jesus, you called blessed all who hear your word and keep it. May the intercession of Mary, first among missionaries, be a source of joy and consolation for missionaries who labor far from home. Relying on your help, we pray:

Presider: God of all peoples, you sent Christ as your life-giving word. Hear our prayers, and by your Spirit help us always to enflesh the gospel that offers true and lasting freedom. We ask this in the name of Jesus.

For the Spread of the Gospel
Option #2

[For the commissioning of missionaries.]

Presider: Let us entrust to God's care the church's ministry of word and sacrament and those who serve the gospel throughout the world.

Petition Leader: Our response today is, **"Receive our prayers, O God."**

Christ was sent by God to reconcile all things through the cross. May all who have been signed with the cross in baptism be ardent witnesses of the gospel. We ask in faith:

Christ promised to be with the disciples until all things reach their fulfillment. May [*Names of missionaries to be commissioned*] experience Christ's presence on the road and in the breaking of bread. We ask in faith:

Christ sent the disciples with the message of salvation. May our sisters and brothers, who leave our midst for the missions, be carriers of Christ's compassion. We ask in faith:

Christ has entrusted the gospel of peace to the church. May God's word, dwelling in our hearts through faith, help build up the lives of peoples plagued by poverty and violence. We ask in faith:

Christ accepted suffering for the sake of all humankind. May missionaries be upheld by the Spirit of Jesus in time of trial and discouragement, especially in hostile environments. We ask in faith:

Christ affirmed the faith and trust that people placed in God's power to save. May the ministries of missionaries affirm the trusting faith of the peoples whose lives they will share. We ask in faith:

Presider: Christ Jesus, you alone have planted the seeds of eternal life among us. They are ours to water through the spread of your gospel. Hear our prayers for blessings as our sisters and brothers take leave. By word and action may all missionaries help your gifts of faith and love to flourish throughout the world. We pray in your name, life-giving Word.

For Retreats (Pastoral or Spiritual Meetings)

Presider: We have come together to be refreshed by the Spirit, so let us entrust this retreat to God's care.

Petition Leader: Our response today is, **"God, renew and bless us!"**

That we may find the word of God to be a lamp to our feet. We ask in faith:

That the Spirit will help us when we do not know how to pray. We ask in faith:

That this time of retreat will be an opportunity to be renewed in body, mind, and spirit. We ask in faith:

That we may grow in self-appreciation and respect for our individual giftedness. We ask in faith:

That the Spirit will enable us to discern ways to use God's gifts for the good of others. We ask in faith:

That we may ponder the legacies of love and faith passed on to us and that inspire us still. We ask in faith:

That the special needs and concerns we bring with us to this retreat may be placed in God's loving care. [Petition leader, please allow a sufficient pause for quiet prayer.] We ask in faith:

Presider: Come Spirit of all grace and peace. Gift us with your presence, lift up our prayer, and bring refreshment to our souls. Make this holy time and holy ground for us. We call you forth in Jesus' name.

Blessing of Human Labor

[These petitions are also suitable for Labor Day, St. Joseph the Worker, Sts. Isidore and Maria, Farmers, or St. Martha.]

Presider: Let our prayers call down God's blessing upon human labor.

Petition Leader: Our response is, **"Bless the work of our hands, O God."**

For the heads of household, especially single parent families; may those who work to feed, clothe, and house children be strengthened by God's care. We pray:

For all in the public work force; may their labor help improve the quality of life for the good of society. We pray:

For those who earn their livelihood as artists; may we continue to value the skills and talents God has given to so many people. We pray:

For all who work in the professions; may the Spirit enable them to live gospel values in the workplace as well as in private life. We pray:

For those who labor in the fields, especially migrant workers and families; may we show ourselves a good society and help to provide for them safe housing, just wages, and quality education. We pray:

For all who are affected by unemployment and struggling against financial ruin; may the Holy Spirit help us to befriend and support others in time of crisis. We pray:

For those who are searching for solutions to unemployment; may the Spirit give us right judgment and wisdom to reach just solutions. We pray:

Presider: God of all creation, you gave to man and woman care for your creation. Through our work may your will be fulfilled. We ask you to accept our prayers through Jesus Christ who, in sharing our humanity, labored as a carpenter.

After the Harvest

[These petitions are also suitable for Thanksgiving Day in the U.S. and Canada.]

Presider: In a spirit of gratitude for material blessings let us uphold in prayer the needs of our world.

Petition Leader: Our prayer response is, **"Gracious God, hear our prayer."**

Creating God, you fashioned the earth and made it suitable for human life. May we use our gifts to make our society a suitable place to uphold all life. We pray:

Sustaining God, you bless the work of our hands and provide for our needs. May we sustain those who are less fortunate than we are. We pray:

Redeeming God, you freed Israel from slavery and led them into a land flowing with milk and honey. Enable us to safeguard human freedoms so that every life may be lived in peace. We pray:

Compassionate God, in Christ you came to the aid of those who knew misery. May our public leaders follow your ways and aid those who suffer. We pray:

Loving God, you filled the earth with natural beauty and plentiful resources. Enable us to care for creation and use wisely and respectfully its natural gifts. We pray:

Just God, you call us to walk humbly in your presence. Give us a spirit of humility and banish all greed and thanklessness from our hearts. We pray:

Healing God, you made the earth bring forth vegetation to help in healing our illnesses. Guide us that we may be instruments of your healing love at all times. We pray:

Presider: Almighty God, Source of all life and goodness, receive our prayers, keep us strong in love and continue to watch over our families, our land, and our nation. Grant this through Christ, our Lord.

For the Hungry of the World
(Peace and Justice, Option #1)

Presider: Jesus is the Living Bread who fills the hungry with good things. Let us pray in his name on behalf of those who lack food.

Petition Leader: In faith we call out, **"Living Bread, hear our prayer!"**

Christ Jesus, we entrust to you the church's work for greater economic justice throughout the world; may your Spirit bless our efforts. We pray:

Jesus, Word of Life, we ask that your transforming grace bring about deeper conversion in our lifestyles; may we turn from apathy and wastefulness. We pray:

Jesus, Bread of Life, we hold up in prayer all who lack basic nourishment; may your church come to the aid of any who are wanting in the basic necessities of life. We pray:

Christ, our Light, we implore you to fill us with the spirit of generosity toward programs that feed the hungry; may soup kitchens, homeless shelters, and other social agencies find strong community support. We pray:

Christ, Sun of Justice, we entrust to you our local, state, and national governments; may our legislators act with justice toward the economically poor, the unemployed, migrant workers, farmers, and food producers. We pray:

Christ, our Peace, we ask you to receive with tender mercy those who have died from lack of food, especially infants and children. We pray:

Christ, our Teacher, we ask continued blessings upon all who work to educate on good nutrition and wise use of our natural resources. We pray:

Presider: God, Giver of Manna, continue to shower the hungry with good things. Fill us with a generous love that we may share our daily bread with the hungry and be pleasing in your sight. Grant this in the name of Jesus, our Bread of Life.

For the Homeless (Peace and Justice, Option #2)

Presider: Let us pray to our God who shelters us with compassion.

Petition Leader: Our response is, **"God, hear our call!"**

As we raise our voices to you in solidarity with those whose human existence is marked by homelessness, rejection, and isolation, we pray:

As we care for those who feel unloved and abandoned, especially infants and children, we pray:

As we work to provide quality housing and health care to the economically poor, we pray:

As we struggle to call our society to be more attentive to the needs of the homeless, we pray:

As we seek your saving grace to break down the barriers of hostility between those who live in economic and political security and those who do not, we pray:

As we invoke your Spirit to bring the grace of conversion to our own hearts, that we may be ever more gracious in showing hospitality to others, we pray:

Presider: Kind and gracious God, in you all the peoples of the earth have a lasting dwelling place. Hear our prayers and help us to extend your care to those most in need. We pray in Jesus' name.

For Those Unjustly Deprived of Liberty
(Peace and Justice, Option #3)

Presider: Let us pray in the freedom of the sons and daughters of God.

Petition Leader: Our response is, **"Protect us by means of truth, O Christ."**

Keep the word of truth in our hearts and upon our lips, that we may proclaim your freeing love to all peoples. Believing in your word, we pray:

Strengthen us by your Spirit, that all may enjoy the freedom of the daughters and sons of God. Believing in the Giver of Life, we pray:

Empower us to safeguard the rights and dignity of persons, especially all who are unjustly deprived of liberty. Believing in your resurrection, we pray:

Plant in our hearts the seeds of unfailing justice, that they may bring forth a harvest of compassion for the most needy among us. Believing you are the Sun of Justice, we pray:

Bless us in our commitment to compassionate living, that through the works of mercy we may be instruments of your peace. Believing in your reconciling love, we pray:

Encourage those whose personal freedoms are denied by unjust laws, systems, or governments, that they may not lose hope. Believing you make all things new, we pray:

Renew the spirit of those psychologically paralyzed from physical abuse and torture. Believing you offer us healing, we pray:

Provide each of us with the gift of persevering prayer, that we may draw our help from you in time of trial. Believing you intercede for us, we pray:

Presider: Our God, our Refuge and our Strength, receive our prayers through your Living Truth who sets us free, Jesus the Christ.

For Peace and Justice
Option #4

Presider: Today let us pray in solidarity with all who are longing for greater peace in our world.

Petition Leader: Our response will be a moment of silent prayer after each petition. [Petition leader, please allow for a sufficient period of silence after each intercession.]

For all who are actively engaged in medical and scientific research, especially those working to develop cures and immunizations for deadly diseases, we pray.

For all who struggle financially to own their own homes and to be self-supporting, we pray.

For immigrants, especially those striving to learn English as a second language so as to participate meaningfully and integrally in our society, we pray.

For all who labor painfully to create new bonds of friendship among enemies, especially in regions torn apart by war, bigotry, and ethnic prejudices, we pray.

For women and children who become sexual victims of terrorists, military personnel, and kidnappers, we pray.

For a deeper commitment to act justly toward laborers from poorer nations who reap little or no profit from the work of their hands, we pray.

For the wisdom to recognize in our lifestyles any greed, wastefulness, or disrespect for the earth's resources, we pray.

For those peace and justice concerns that are important to us individually, let us now pray quietly.

Presider: God, in the richness of your compassion hear our prayers and help us create a world where your Spirit of loving kindness flourishes. We ask this in the name of Jesus Christ, who lives and reigns with you and the Spirit, forever.

For Peace and Justice
Option #5

Presider: Prompted by the Holy Spirit of peace, let us pray to be instruments of peace and compassion.

Petition Leader: Our prayer response today is, **"Christ, our Justice, hear our prayer."**

That we may all have a love for justice that serves the most needy and neglected among us, we pray:

That we may be stirred by your Wisdom to pursue integrity of word and deed in our lives, we pray:

That we may be empowered to renew ourselves constantly through prayer and personal conversion as a witness to faith in your gospel, we pray:

That we may strive with greater courage to create inclusive communities of compassion that renew the hopes of the poor, we pray:

That we may continuously commit ourselves to be at peace with all creation, we pray:

That we may address the causes of violence and greed in our world with light drawn from your gospel, we pray:

That we may hear the voice of the Spirit calling us to work for greater unity and respect among all races, nations, cultures, and faith traditions, we pray:

Presider: Gracious God, receive the prayers we make this day in the name of the One who is for us the Dawn of Justice and Desire of Nations, Jesus Christ, who lives and reigns forever and ever.

For Respect for Life

Presider: Our faith in Christ's resurrection affirms God's gift of life. Let us pray to be rich in our commitment to God's sacred gift.

Petition Leader: Our prayer response today is, **"Giver of Life, fill us with love."**

God birthed creation out of love. May our reverence for all life and creation express our respect for the divine will. Moved by God's Spirit, we pray:

God calls us to choose between life and death. May all who choose life for themselves choose it for the unborn as well. Moved by God's Spirit, we pray:

God restored our life through Christ, the Healer. May the church's ministries and sacraments sustain in hope the terminally ill and any who are suicidal. Moved by God's Spirit, we pray:

Christ came as the Word of consolation not condemnation. May Christians in public office use their influence to reverse legislation that permits termination of human life for any reason, including the death penalty. Moved by God's Spirit, we pray:

Christ promised to be our Advocate before the face of God. May we be advocates for nonviolence and stand against government-subsidized programs and schools that train others to kill. Moved by God's Spirit, we pray:

The Spirit, who parents the poor, has been given to us. May the Spirit empower us to address the causes of poverty, abuse, and illness that deprive people of life, especially for infants, women, and the elderly poor. Moved by God's Spirit, we pray:

Presider: God of perfect peace, violence and cruelty obscure your love for the world. May we follow the way of compassion and forgiveness that reveals your kindness and care and grow in our respect for life. We ask this in the name of Jesus, your living Word of love.

Beginning of an Academic Year
(Junior/Senior High School)

Presider: Let us ask for the Holy Spirit's guidance as we begin this school year.

Petition Leader: Our response is, **"Holy Spirit, be with us."**

For the faculty, students, and employees of [*Name of school*]. May each person's blessings be used for the good of the whole school community. We pray:

For new faculty and students. May they experience welcome, and may the rest of us be quick to extend hospitality and help. We pray:

For a spirit of friendship and cooperation. May we work together to support and care for each other in the Spirit of Jesus. We pray:

For the gift of knowledge and understanding. May the Holy Spirit give us the intellectual, physical, and spiritual gifts we need to grow as whole persons. We pray:

For the gift of personal responsibility. May we use wisely the opportunities that come our way for learning and for doing good. We pray:

For those who have been entrusted with leadership of the school. May [*Name of the principal or administrators*] know God's grace and blessings. We pray:

For the school's benefactors and all who make it possible for us to be here. May their generosity and the willingness of our parents to invest in our education be recognized as gifts from God. We pray:

Presider: Good and gracious God, hear our prayers and help us to grow in wisdom and grace. May we always use wisely the gifts you give us in this life. Grant our prayers in the name of Jesus Christ, who lives and reigns with you and the Holy Spirit, one God forever and ever.

Baccalaureate Mass

Presider: On this special occasion, let us pray in a spirit of joyful hope.

Petition Leader: Our prayer response is, **"Lord, be with us."**

For the church as it moves forth in faith with its heart set on God's kingdom. May it continue to place its gifts in service of all peoples. We call on Christ and ask:

For the world composed of so many wonderful races, nations and cultures. May each of us do our part in helping it dwell in security and peace. We call on Christ and ask:

[For an eighth-grade graduation.]
For ourselves as we take leave of [*Name of school*]. May the Spirit of knowledge and understanding guide us as we continue our learning in high school. We call on Christ and ask:

[For a high-school graduation.]
For ourselves as we take leave of [*Name of school*]. May God's Spirit guide us in right paths and help us to put to good use our personal gifts and education. We call on Christ and ask:

[For a college graduation or other academic circumstance.]
For ourselves as we celebrate the joy of this moment. May the future be for us a time of continuous learning, helping to care for the common good and growing spiritually rich in the sight of God. We call on Christ and ask:

For those who have served us as teachers [*and counselors/mentors*]. May the Spirit of God continue to inspire their dedication and commitment to education. We call on Christ and ask:

For all of us who have gathered to give thanks at this holy table. May we be ever grateful to God for the saving gift of Jesus Christ. We call on Christ and ask:

For our families and friends who have supported us during these years of study. May those who have offered us encouragement along the way be blessed abundantly. We call on Christ and ask:

For those who are no longer with us yet remain alive in our hearts. May our deceased relatives and friends (especially _____) know the enduring peace of Christ. We call on Christ and ask:

Presider: God in heaven, hear the prayers of those who call on you. Sustain in us the grace and peace of Christ that our life's journey will lead us to everlasting life. We ask this in the name of Jesus Christ.

Dedication of a Church

Presider: Because we are a living temple for God in the Spirit, let us invoke the grace and peace of Jesus Christ for the church and the world.

Petition Leader: Our prayer response is, **"God, graciously hear us."**

For the Catholic church together with Pope [*Name*] and the world's bishops, may your faithful people be filled with the Holy Spirit's life and gifts. Rejoicing in God, our Savior, we pray:

For the Archdiocese/Diocese of [*Name*] and our bishop [*Name*], may the church in this locale continue to proclaim the glories of God in word and sacrament. Rejoicing in God, our Savior, we pray:

For this parish community together with our pastor [*Name*], may our faith, hope, and love flourish through the intercession and protection of Mary (and _____ [the name of the church's patron may be included here]). Rejoicing in God, our Savior, we pray:

For all who enter these doors in search of God's peace and healing love, may they find us to be a rich haven of compassion and a vibrant community of faith in the risen Christ. Rejoicing in God, our Savior, we pray:

For all who will proclaim God's word here and celebrate the sacraments of life, may those who minister in our midst be received as instruments of Christ's love for the church. Rejoicing in God, our Savior, we pray:

For all who have helped to build this house of prayer because of their love for God and the church, may their generosity and dedication be pleasing in God's sight. Rejoicing in God, our Savior, we pray:

For ourselves who proclaim the dying and rising of the Lord at this table of unity, may the eucharist be the center of our lives together. Rejoicing in God, our Savior, we pray:

For our beloved dead who longed for the heavenly temple, may they be found praising God in the company of the angels and saints. Rejoicing in God, our Savior, we pray:

Presider: God ever gracious and kind, receive our prayers, and by the power of your Holy Spirit keep us united in Christ, who intercedes for us at your right hand. Grant this through Christ, our Lord.

Dedication of a Chapel (or New Altar) in a Health-Care Facility

Presider: Having received the Word of Life that proclaims God's enduring love, let us seek God's grace and peace for all humankind.

Petition Leader: Our prayer response today is, **"God, rich in mercy, hear us."**

God of our ancestors, you sent prophets to call Israel back to yourself. Through the church's proclamation of the gospel may all peoples be drawn to the healing love of Christ. Remembering your steadfast love, we pray:

God of the poor and lowly, you sent Christ to announce your favor to the sick and the broken-hearted. May all who call on you in this holy space find solace and strength. Remembering your steadfast love, we pray:

God, source of every blessing, you brought healing to the world through the life-giving death of Jesus. May all who join in Christ's sacrifice of praise at this holy table know your saving power in their lives. Remembering your steadfast love, we pray:

God, you sent your anointing Spirit to complete the work of Jesus. May all who serve in this [*hospital/residence/facility/etc.*] be channels of the Spirit's power. Remembering your steadfast love, we pray:

God, you give us the oil of gladness through the healing touch of Christ. May all who call on you in faith as they celebrate the sacraments of life be blessed with your help, forgiveness, and peace. Remembering your steadfast love, we pray:

God of the living and the dead, you receive us with mercy when our life on earth has ended. Take into your embrace all who leave this world longing for the New Jerusalem where every tear is wiped away. Remembering your steadfast love, we pray:

Presider: God, abounding in kindness and compassion, receive our prayers and keep alive in us a vibrant faith in your redeeming love. May all who call on you in Spirit and truth in this place of prayer [or *at this sacred table*], be sustained in your grace. Grant this through Christ, our Lord.

Civic Holidays

Birth of Dr. Martin Luther King, Jr.

Presider: Through the Holy Spirit God gathers into the one body of Christ persons of every race, language, and culture. Let us call upon the Spirit of unity and peace to be with us and all peoples of goodwill.

Petition Leader: Our prayer response today is, **"Come, Spirit of peace."**

God announced through the prophets a time when old and young would dream together. May the Holy Spirit continue to inspire in all people the desire for world peace. We pray:

Christ abolished the barrier of hostility between Jew and Greek through the cross of salvation. May Christ's Spirit continue to prompt the church to work for unity and respect among peoples and an end to racism. We pray:

Christ freed us from slavery to sin and death. May all who enjoy the freedom of God's children by baptism work to break every form of oppression that plagues human lives. We pray:

The Spirit of Wisdom prepares one table at which her children may feast. May all who are nourished on Word and sacraments be faithful to the Truth that re-creates us in Christ. We pray:

Christ promised that the Holy Spirit would sustain us in time of trial. May the Spirit's strength be with all who labor for human rights, especially in hostile environments. We pray:

Filled with the Holy Spirit, Mary praised the love of God that raises up the lowly. Under her patronage may our nation and its leaders grow strong in their defense of human life and civil rights. We pray:

Presider: God of all creation, we echo the words of St. Peter, "Truly, your love shows no partiality." We praise your goodness that has given us life and raised us up in Christ. Receive our prayers, and by the one Spirit of love may we move forward to the kingdom, where Jesus is Lord forever and ever.

Memorial Day (U.S.)

[The following petitions are suitable when a Mass for the Dead is celebrated on this civic holiday. Since it frequently occurs during the Easter season these petitions are written to celebrate the resurrection.]

Presider: As we set aside this day to cherish the legacies of love and faith that others have left behind, let us pray to be filled with the same life-giving gifts that are given in the name of the risen Christ.

Petition Leader: Our prayer response today is, **"Merciful God, hear our prayer."**

God raised Jesus from the dead and has bestowed on him the name above all other names. May the dead for whom we offer this eucharist be given eternal life in the name of Jesus. We pray:

God has removed the veil that covered the peoples by stripping death of its power. May all who labor to safeguard human rights and life be sustained by the Spirit of Jesus. We pray:

God has revealed Jesus to be the Dawn of eternal light. May all Christians walk by the light of the gospel until they arrive at the New Jerusalem. We pray:

God has sent Christ as a peace offering for our sins. May we continue to experience God's reconciling love in our lives that we may be instruments of peace in the lives of others. We pray:

God sent Christ as the Living Bread come down from heaven. May we who celebrate the dying and rising of Christ at this table be filled with the hope of coming to the feast of life in heaven. We pray:

God has remembered the lowly and deposed the mighty. Through the care Mary shows the church by her love and prayers, may the poor and forgotten among us be clothed in the Spirit's love. We pray:

Presider: God, indeed your love fills us with good things in the name of Jesus. May the dead be filled with eternal life and may we, your pilgrim church, continue to enjoy the Spirit's gifts. Grant our prayers in Jesus' name.

Victoria Day (Canada)

Presider: Let us seek God's help as we pray on this national holiday.

Petition Leader: Our prayer response today is, **"Lord, guide and bless us."**

For the church as it professes its faith in God's saving love; may the people of God in Christ imbue society with the life-giving truths of faith. We pray:

For all who serve in public office; may our elected officials and heads of state, especially [*Name of Prime Minister*], be blessed with wisdom and integrity as they fulfill their duties. We pray:

For our country so rich in diversity and beauty; may the many peoples of Canada be united in ideals and a common love for human flourishing. We pray:

For the economically poor among us; may those who are brought low by financial problems and unemployment find strong support in their time of need. We pray:

For a rebirth of moral integrity and spiritual values in our society; may the Holy Spirit fill us with a love for God that inspires living justly and honorably all our days. We pray:

For the gift of healing wherever alienation and hurt exists in our land; may we come to know the Spirit's power drawing us together in peace and unity. We pray:

Presider: God in heaven, Creator of all, you call all peoples on earth to serve you. Hear our prayers, bless our country, and fill your people with every grace and blessing, in Jesus' name.

Canada Day

Presider: Grateful for the gift of freedom that comes to us through the goodness of God, let us pray that our nation may use wisely every blessing it receives.

Petition Leader: Our response today is, **"Lord, hear our prayer."**

For the Catholic church in Canada; may the Canadian bishops, clergy, and the faithful labor tirelessly on behalf of human rights that all may enjoy the goods of God's creation. We ask in faith:

For the leaders of our national and provincial governments; may their service to the people of Canada be marked by personal integrity and the highest ethical principles. We ask in faith:

For all who serve in the country's judicial systems; may the laws and rights they uphold never neglect the fundamental right to life for all persons. We ask in faith:

For all who have dedicated their lives to the pursuit of the common good; may their works of justice be pleasing in God's sight and brought to perfection in the one sacrifice of Christ. We ask in faith:

For persons who do not experience the fullness of freedom in our midst because of racism, sexism, greed, and indifference; may their call for true equality and justice for all find an echo in our hearts. We ask in faith:

For all who labor to preserve our natural resources and nature's beauty; may their efforts help inspire all Canadians to grow in their respect for life and creation. We ask in faith:

For ourselves who praise God's goodness in this holy meal; may we be generous in showing hospitality to all who come to this land in the hope of starting a new life. We ask in faith:

Presider: God of love, Abba of Jesus, hear our prayers. Bestow your Spirit on us that we may act with reverence and compassion, and our nation abide in your peace. Grant this through Christ, our Lord.

Independence Day (U.S.)

Presider: Grateful for the gift of freedom that comes to us through the goodness of God, let us pray that our nation may use wisely every blessing it receives.

Petition Leader: Our response today is, **"Lord, hear our prayer."**

For the Catholic Church in the United States; may the American bishops, clergy, and the faithful labor tirelessly on behalf of human rights that all may enjoy the goods of God's creation. We ask in faith:

For the leaders of our national government; may their service to the people of the United States be marked by personal integrity and the highest ethical principles. We ask in faith:

For all who serve in the country's judicial systems; may the laws and rights they uphold never neglect the fundamental right to life for all persons, including the unborn and persons convicted of crimes of violence. We ask in faith:

For all who have labored to secure and preserve human freedoms; may their efforts be pleasing in God's sight and brought to perfection in the one sacrifice of Christ. We ask in faith:

For persons who do not experience the fullness of freedom in our midst because of racism, sexism, greed, and indifference; may their call for true equality and justice for all find an echo in our hearts. We ask in faith:

For all who have died with their hope set on a heavenly homeland where peace endures forever; may all people of goodwill who acted in faith find rest from their labors. We ask in faith:

For ourselves who praise God's goodness in this holy meal; may we be generous in showing hospitality to all who come to this land in the hope of finding new life. We ask in faith:

Presider: God of love, Abba of Jesus, hear our prayers. Bestow your Spirit on us that we may act with reverence and compassion, and our nation abide in your peace. Grant this through Christ, our Lord.

Thanksgiving Day (U.S. and Canada)

[For another option see "After the Harvest," page 188.]

Presider: In a spirit of thanksgiving let us pray to the Sustainer of Life for the spiritual and material blessings that dignify life.

Petition Leader: Our prayer response today is, **"God of blessing, hear our prayer."**

For the church as it renders daily thanks at the table of the eucharist; may our love for Christ be witnessed in our dedication to live honorably and respectfully. With grateful hearts, we ask:

For all who will gather to share a common meal with family and friends today; may our sharing of food lead us to share our blessings with the human family. With grateful hearts, we ask:

For the homeless and the hungry in our midst; may their want and need move others to share generously from their surplus of love and material blessings. With grateful hearts, we ask:

For Native Americans, who revere this land as their native soil; may their efforts to live in the Spirit of freedom and respect find strong support in the hearts of all people of goodwill. With grateful hearts, we ask:

For our land which God has endowed with immense beauty and resources; may we come to live in harmony with all creation and abandon all forms of wastefulness. With grateful hearts, we ask:

For all whose lives are built on the immigration and journeys of our ancestors; may their legacies of courageous faith and hope inspire us to safeguard the freedoms for which they labored. With grateful hearts, we ask:

For families who feel the absence of a loved one on this holiday; may those who mourn find their spirit nourished in remembering God's mercy. With grateful hearts, we ask:

Presider: God, ever generous and kind, you are the source of every blessing. Hear our prayers and fill your people with gifts that draw us to you, through Christ, our Savior.

U.S. Civic Holiday (General)

Presider: Let us pray in the Spirit of peace for our society and the poor among us.

Petition Leader: Our response to our intercessions today is, **"Christ, our Peace, hear us!"**

That the seeds of peace and justice sown by our ancestors will bear fruit in our continued commitment to serve the poor, the sick, and the needy of our times. We ask:

That the legacy of love left to us by past generations of immigrants will inspire us to be generous in offering hospitality to new immigrants. We ask:

That the leaders of our nation and of religious bodies in the U.S. will pursue serious collaboration in securing health care for every citizen and resident alien. We ask:

That each of us may have a genuine respect for our natural resources and cultivate lifestyles that will ensure future generations access to the beauty of creation. We ask:

That employers will manifest increasing justice toward all workers, especially toward women in the work force. We ask:

That our celebration of the eucharist on this [*Name of civic holiday*] will move the Catholic community in the United States to foster communities rich in compassion toward the homeless, the unemployed, the disabled, the hungry, and the alienated. We ask:

Presider: God of everlasting goodness, receive our prayers and help our nation to flourish as a land of liberty and justice for all. Grant this through Christ, our Peacemaker with you.

Miscellaneous Petitions and Special Commemorations

Miscellaneous Petitions

[The singular petitions in this section may be integrated or adapted into any of the intercessions as the need arises. The bracketed names of saints following the petition are occasions when the petition may be used.]

For a New Bishop (Before Appointment)

Let us entrust to the Holy Spirit the Archdiocese/Diocese of [*Name*] as it awaits its new bishop. May the Spirit guide the discernment of Pope [*Name*] and all involved in the selection of bishops. We pray:

For a New Bishop or Pastor (After Appointment)

Let us entrust to the Holy Spirit our new Archbishop/Bishop/Pastor [*Name*] that his ministry to and guidance of the Archdiocese/Diocese/Parish of [*Name*] may be blessed with spiritual richness. We pray:

For a New Principal (Before Appointment)

We ask the Holy Spirit to guide the deliberations of all involved in selecting a new principal for [*Name of school*]. May their discernment be blessed with wisdom and foresight. We pray:

For a New Principal (After Appointment)

We ask the Holy Spirit to guide the ministry of service and education of [*Name*] as the new principal of [*Name of school*]. May this school community be blessed because of his/her leadership. We pray:

For a Parish Retreat or Mission

Let us entrust to the Holy Spirit our parish retreat/mission. Through the working of grace may it be a time of spiritual renewal and blessing. We pray:

For Artists and Entertainers

May all artists and entertainers be blessed with a spirit of gratitude to God for their gifts, remembering that all humanity is God's work of art in Christ. We pray:

[St. Clare of Assisi, August 11]

For Athletes

For all athletes, may God grant them health in body and spirit with their hearts set on everlasting life as the greatest victory of all. We pray:

[St. Sebastian, January 20]

For Charitable Societies

We ask God to bestow abundant blessings upon all charitable societies, especially those that help relieve human suffering. With confident faith, we pray:

[St. Vincent de Paul, September 27]

For Engaged Couples

We entrust to the Spirit's guidance couples preparing for marriage. May they prepare for this sacrament of love with maturity and a spirit of self-giving. We pray:

For Fathers

May God's love fill the lives of all fathers and bless them with the grace and peace of Christ. We pray:

May God console the hearts of all fathers who have suffered the loss of a child. Trusting in God's compassion for the grieving, we pray:

May God bless all men who extend a father's love to others, especially those who care for the young. We pray:

May God receive with tender mercy our fathers who have died. We pray:

[Father's Day or St. Joseph, March 19]

For Firefighters

We entrust to God's protection and care all who serve their communities as firefighters. May they be kept safe as they work to protect others from harm. We pray:

[St. Catherine of Siena, April 29]

For Fishermen/women

May all who labor at fishing be sustained by God's grace and protected in their work. With gratitude to God for all good gifts, we pray:

[St. Andrew the Apostle, November 30]

For Lawyers and Judges

For all who serve society as lawyers and judges. May they perform their work in fidelity to justice and honesty ever mindful of God's law of love. We pray:

[St. Thomas More, June 22]

For Married Couples

We ask God's blessing upon all marriages. May the vows of love spouses promised on the day of their marriage continue to deepen and be a source of joy for the church and society. We pray:

For Medical Professionals and Health-Care Personnel
For all whose lives are dedicated to the care of the sick, especially doctors and nurses. May they be instruments of God's compassion and manifest a commitment to the gift of life. We pray:
[St. John of God, March 8, or St. Elizabeth of Hungary, November 17]

For Military Personnel
For all who serve in the military; may they perform their duties with moral integrity and dedication to protecting our nation, that it may abide in peace. We pray:
[St. Martin of Tours, November 11]

For Missing Persons
We ask Christ, who came to seek out the lost, to guard and protect all missing persons, especially children. May they be restored in good health to their loved ones. Relying on God's help, we pray:

For Mothers
May God's love fill the lives of all mothers and bless them with the grace and peace of Christ. We pray:

May God console the hearts of all mothers who have suffered the loss of a child. Trusting in God's compassion for the grieving, we pray:

May God bless all women who extend a mother's love to others, especially those who care for the young. We pray:

May God receive with tender mercy all mothers who have died. We pray:
[Mother's Day, or St. Monica, August 27]

For New Families or Individuals in the Parish
For all families and individuals who have recently joined our parish family. May they experience among us the hospitality of Christ and feel welcomed as sisters and brothers in the Lord. We pray:

For Orphans and Abandoned Children
We embrace in prayer children who are orphans, especially those who have been abandoned by their parents. May Christian communities never cease to be havens of compassion and love for homeless children. We pray:
[St. John Bosco, January 31;
St. Jerome Emiliani, February 8;
or St. Frances Cabrini, November 13]

For a Parish Catechetical Program

For our parish religious education program. May this ministry of education enjoy the favors of the Holy Spirit that all may grow in their knowledge and love of God. We pray:

[St. Charles Borromeo, November 4]

For Parish Hospice Workers and Volunteers

For members of our parish who serve as hospice personnel, volunteers, and aides. May they know God's strength in their ministry to the dying. We pray:

[St. Camillus de Lellis, July 14]

For Peace in Time of War or Other Disturbances

[See also "For Peace and Justice."]

For an end to all violence and hatred that we may live free from fear of destruction to human life, our homes, and our country/city/land. We pray:

For Person(s) Entering Religious Life From the Parish

May the Holy Spirit, who inspires every good intention, be with [*Name(s)*] as he/she/they begin his/her/their formation for religious life. Relying on God's help in all things, we ask:

For Persons Who Work Under Hazardous Conditions

Let us pray for those who work under hazardous conditions. May God protect them from all harm and sustain in them good health. We pray:

For Physical Safety

May God keep us safe from accidents and all physical harm that we may enjoy good health and well-being all our days. Relying on God to protect us, we pray:

For Police Officers

We ask God's blessing upon all who serve their communities as police officers. May they perform their duties with integrity and respect for every citizen's welfare. We pray:

[St. Michael, September 29]

For Productive Land

We ask God to bless our land and our labor that it may yield a rich harvest, mindful that our lives are meant to yield a harvest of justice in God's sight. We pray:

[Sts. Isidore & Maria, Farmers, May 15]

For Protection From Storms and Natural Disasters

We entrust our well-being and safety to God that we may be surrounded by the divine protection in times of storms and natural disasters. We pray:

For Recovery From a Natural Disaster

For all who have been affected by [*Description and location of disaster*]. May they draw strength from God and the community's support as they work toward recovery. Trusting in God's help, we pray:

For Seminarian(s) From the Parish

Let us hold in prayer [*Name(s)*], [*a seminarian* or *seminarians*] from our parish. May the Holy Spirit guide him/them in these years of study and preparation for the priesthood. We pray:

For Students Leaving for College

We ask God to watch over and bless all youths from our parish community who are leaving for college. May their faith deepen during this year of study. We ask in faith:

For Travelers

Remembering that God watches over our coming and going, we ask that all travelers may arrive safely at their destinations. Trusting in God's care for us, we pray:

[Archangels, September 29]

For Youth Ministers/Youth Ministry

We entrust to God's care and guidance our youth ministry program (and parish youth minister(s) [*Name(s)*]). May this service to our young people be spiritually rich. We pray:

[St. Aloysius Gonzaga, June 21]

Special Commemorations

Anniversary of Ordination or Installation (A Bishop)

We entrust to God's care, Bishop [*Name*], on the anniversary of his episcopal ordination/installation. May the grace and peace of Christ and the love of God continue to sustain his ministry to God's people of the church of [*Name*]. We pray:

Anniversary of Ordination (A Priest)
We entrust to God's care Father [Name] on the anniversary of his priestly ordination. May God's Spirit uphold him in his ministry among God's people. We pray:

Anniversary of Ordination (A Deacon)
We ask God's blessing upon Deacon [Name] on the anniversary of his ordination to the diaconate. May his ministry of service continue to enjoy the grace and peace of Christ. We pray:

Anniversary of Marriage (Twenty-Fifth or Fiftieth)
We ask God's continued blessings upon all marriages and in particular [Names] as they celebrate their twenty-fifth/fiftieth anniversary. May their love more and more abound to the glory of God. Relying on God's goodness, we pray:

Anniversary of Religious Profession or Reception (Twenty-Fifth or Fiftieth)
We rejoice with [Name(s)] on this twenty-fifth/fiftieth jubilee and entrust him/her/them to God's loving care. May the Spirit bring to completion the good God has begun in him/her/them. Trusting in God's love for us, we pray:

Anniversary of Death
We remember [Name] on this anniversary of his/her death. Through the mercy of God may he/she rejoice in the company of the saints in light. We ask in faith:

Anniversary of a Dedication of a Church
Grateful to God for this house of worship, we ask on this anniversary of its dedication that it may continue to be a home for the church and place of prayer for all peoples, to God's honor and glory. We pray:

On a Patronal Feast Day
[On a feast of the BVM or a saint.]
For [Name] on his/her patronal feast day, may the intercession of [Name] bring the blessings of Christ in the Spirit to rest upon him/her. We pray:

Remembering that God calls each of us by name, we entrust [Name] to the divine care on his/her feast day. May the rich gifts of the Spirit be his/hers in abundance. We pray:

Litanies and Prayer Services

Litany of the Holy Spirit

[Format #1, a novena of prayer for an assembly]

[The following litany might be used as a novena of prayer in preparation for Pentecost. It could begin on the Friday after Ascension Day and conclude on Saturday the vigil of Pentecost. It may also be adapted for use at other times throughout the liturgical year. When it is used at the end of a eucharistic celebration the scriptural proclamation may be omitted. The format presented here is for an assembly and arranged for nine days. The opening is used to begin each day's prayer.]

Opening

Presider or Leader: [after the customary greeting of the assembly] Let us hear the word of God that we may be moved to prayer.

Proclamation of the Word: [The reading is proclaimed in the customary manner with the appropriate conclusion, "The word of the Lord."]

> Day One: 2 Timothy 1:5-8a
> Day Two: Galatians 5:22-23a, 24-25
> Day Three: Ephesians 1:3-4
> Day Four: Titus 3:4-7
> Day Five: Romans 8:14-17
> Day Six: 1 Corinthians 12:4-7
> Day Seven: Ephesians 4:1-3
> Day Eight: Romans 8:26-27
> Day Nine: 1 Corinthians 12:12-13; John 14:15-17

Presider or Leader: Let us invoke the Holy Spirit.

[The litany continues with the prayers and responses from the specific days as found on the following pages.]

Day One

[Presider or leader begins with the opening from text above.]

Presider or Leader: Come, Holy Spirit, Gift of God most high. Kindle in us the fire of your love.

Assembly:
Kindle in us the fire of reverence.
Kindle in us the fire of nonviolence.
Kindle in us the fire of tenderness.
Kindle in us the fire of fidelity.
Kindle in us the fire of humility.

Kindle in us the fire of conversion.
Kindle in us the fire of unceasing praise.
Kindle in us the fire of persevering prayer.
Kindle in us the fire of unfailing justice.
Kindle in us the fire of generosity.

[A single candle may be lighted from the Paschal candle followed by a brief period of quiet reflection. At the end of the period of silence, the presider or leader continues:]

Presider or Leader: The Spirit God gives is no cowardly spirit.
Assembly: Let us stir into flame the gift of God bestowed on us.

Presider or Leader: Let us pray as Jesus taught:
Assembly: Our Father . . .

Presider or Leader: Loving God, may the Spirit whom you send to be our Helper and Friend kindle in our hearts the fire of love. Keep your church attentive to the Spirit's voice that all peoples may be consoled by the light of truth. Grant this through Jesus Christ, our Redeemer, who lives and reigns with you and the Holy Spirit, one God forever and ever.

[The prayer may conclude with a blessing or in the absence of a priest or minister with the following:]

Presider or Leader: Let us bless our God
Assembly: And render thanks always. Amen.

Day Two

[Presider or leader begins with the opening from page 216. The single candle lighted on the previous day is lit from the beginning of the following prayer.]

Presider or Leader: Come, Holy Spirit, Giver of Life. Kindle in us the fire of your love.

Assembly:
Kindle in us the strength of the heart of Christ.
Kindle in us the strength to proclaim the Truth.
Kindle in us the strength to be chaste.
Kindle in us the strength to live unselfishly.
Kindle in us the strength to safeguard human freedom.
Kindle in us the strength to stand with the economically poor.
Kindle in us the strength to companion the dying.
Kindle in us the strength to confront racism.

Kindle in us the strength to confront sexism.
Kindle in us the strength to bear wrongs patiently.

[Another single candle may be lighted from the Paschal candle followed by a brief period of quiet reflection. At the end of the period of silence, the presider or leader continues:]

Presider or Leader: The Spirit God gives is no listless spirit.
Assembly: Let us stir into flame the gift of God bestowed on us.

Presider or Leader: Let us pray as Jesus taught:
Assembly: Our Father . . .

Presider or Leader: Loving God, may the Spirit whom you send to be our Helper and Friend kindle in our hearts the fire of love. Keep your church attentive to the Spirit's voice that all peoples may be consoled by the light of truth. Grant this through Jesus Christ, our Redeemer, who lives and reigns with you and the Holy Spirit, one God forever and ever.

[The prayer may conclude with a blessing or in the absence of a priest or minister with the following:]

Presider or Leader: Let us bless our God
Assembly: And render thanks always. Amen.

Day Three

[Presider or leader begins with the opening from page 216. The two candles lighted on the previous day are lit from the beginning of the following prayer.]

Presider or Leader: Come, Holy Spirit, Giver of every good gift. Kindle in us the fire of your love.
Assembly:
  Kindle in us the gift of faith.
  Kindle in us the gift of hope.
  Kindle in us the gift of discernment.
  Kindle in us the gift of wonder.
  Kindle in us the gift of healing.
  Kindle in us the gift of listening.
  Kindle in us the gift of joy.
  Kindle in us the gift of respect for creation.
  Kindle in us the gift of kindness.
  Kindle in us the gift of surrender to God's will.

[Another single candle may be lighted from the Paschal candle followed by a brief period of quiet reflection. At the end of the period of silence, the presider or leader continues:]

Presider or Leader: The Spirit God gives is no hostile spirit.
Assembly: Let us stir into flame the gift of God bestowed on us.

Presider or Leader: Let us pray as Jesus taught:
Assembly: Our Father . . .

Presider or Leader: Loving God, may the Spirit whom you send to be our Helper and Friend kindle in our hearts the fire of love. Keep your church attentive to the Spirit's voice that all peoples may be consoled by the light of truth. Grant this through Jesus Christ, our Redeemer, who lives and reigns with you and the Holy Spirit, one God forever and ever.

[The prayer may conclude with a blessing or in the absence of a priest or minister with the following:]

Presider or Leader: Let us bless our God
Assembly: And render thanks always. Amen.

Day Four

[Presider or leader begins with the opening from page 216. The three candles lighted on the previous days are lit from the beginning of the following prayer.]

Presider or Leader: Come, Holy Spirit, Cause of our inspiration. Kindle in us the fire of your love.

Assembly:
  Kindle in us holy boldness.
  Kindle in us a sacred restlessness.
  Kindle in us a desire for the greater gifts.
  Kindle in us a passion for mercy.
  Kindle in us an unfailing respect for life.
  Kindle in us a love for simplicity.
  Kindle in us a love for Wisdom.
  Kindle in us a new Pentecost of peace.
  Kindle in us a longing for the New Jerusalem.
  Kindle in us the splendor of the Incarnate Word.

[Another single candle may be lighted from the Paschal candle followed by a brief period of quiet reflection. At the end of the period of silence, the presider or leader continues:]

Presider or Leader: The Spirit God gives is no unholy spirit.
Assembly: Let us stir into flame the gift of God bestowed on us.

Presider or Leader: Let us pray as Jesus taught:
Assembly: Our Father . . .

Presider or Leader: Loving God, may the Spirit whom you send to be our Helper and Friend kindle in our hearts the fire of love. Keep your church attentive to the Spirit's voice that all peoples may be consoled by the light of truth. Grant this through Jesus Christ, our Redeemer, who lives and reigns with you and the Holy Spirit, one God forever and ever.

[The prayer may conclude with a blessing or in the absence of a priest or minister with the following:]

Presider or Leader: Let us bless our God
Assembly: And render thanks always. Amen.

Day Five

[Presider or leader begins with the opening from page 216. The four candles lighted on the previous days are lit from the beginning of the following prayer.]

Presider or Leader: Come, Holy Spirit, Source of our freedom. Kindle in us the fire of your love.

Assembly:
Kindle in us a freedom from fear.
Kindle in us a freedom from timidity.
Kindle in us a freedom from all jealousy.
Kindle in us a freedom to imagine.
Kindle in us a freedom to live with imperfections.
Kindle in us a freedom to embrace incompleteness in others.
Kindle in us a freedom from possessiveness.
Kindle in us a freedom to be in solidarity with the poor.
Kindle in us a freedom to let go of old hurts.
Kindle in us a freedom to move forward and not look back.

[Another single candle may be lighted from the Paschal Candle followed by a brief period of quiet reflection. At the end of the period of silence, the presider or leader continues:]

Presider or Leader: The Spirit God gives is no oppressive spirit.
Assembly: Let us stir into flame the gift of God bestowed on us.

Presider or Leader: Let us pray as Jesus taught:
Assembly: Our Father . . .

Presider or Leader: Loving God, may the Spirit whom you send to be our Helper and Friend kindle in our hearts the fire of love. Keep your church attentive to the Spirit's voice that all peoples may be consoled by the light of truth. Grant this through Jesus Christ, our Redeemer, who lives and reigns with you and the Holy Spirit, one God forever and ever.

[The prayer may conclude with a blessing or in the absence of a priest or minister with the following:]

Presider or Leader: Let us bless our God
Assembly: And render thanks always. Amen.

Day Six

[Presider or leader begins with the opening from page 216. The five candles lighted on the previous days are lit from the beginning of the following prayer.]

Presider or Leader: Come, sanctifying Spirit, our soul's delightful guest. Kindle in us the fire of your love.

Assembly:
  Kindle in Pope [*Name*] the gift of holiness.
  Kindle in all bishops the gift of love for your people.
  Kindle in all priests the gift of selflessness.
  Kindle in all deacons the gift of service.
  Kindle in all religious the gift of fidelity.
  Kindle in all theologians the gift of wisdom.
  Kindle in all catechists the gift of knowledge.
  Kindle in all lay ministers the gift of prayer.
  Kindle in all missionaries the gift of zeal.
  Kindle in all your people the gift of unity.

[Another single candle may be lighted from the Paschal candle followed by a brief period of quiet reflection. At the end of the period of silence, the presider or leader continues:]

Presider or Leader: The Spirit God gives is no arrogant spirit.
Assembly: Let us stir into flame the gift of God bestowed on us.

Presider or Leader: Let us pray as Jesus taught:
Assembly: Our Father . . .

Presider or Leader: Loving God, may the Spirit whom you send to be our Helper and Friend kindle in our hearts the fire of love. Keep your church attentive to the Spirit's voice that all peoples may be consoled by the light of truth. Grant this through Jesus Christ, our Redeemer, who lives and reigns with you and the Holy Spirit, one God forever and ever.

[The prayer may conclude with a blessing or in the absence of a priest or minister with the following:]

Presider or Leader: Let us bless our God

Assembly: And render thanks always. Amen.

Day Seven

[Presider or leader begins with the opening from page 216. The six candles lighted on the previous days are lit from the beginning of the following prayer.]

Presider or Leader: Come, consoling Spirit, Light Divine. Kindle in us the fire of your love.

Assembly:
  Kindle in all spouses the gift of fidelity.
  Kindle in all families the gift of peace.
  Kindle in all parents the gift of tenderness.
  Kindle in all children the gift of respect.
  Kindle in all who grieve the gift of consolation.
  Kindle in all who are engaged the gift of discernment.
  Kindle in all who are lonely the gift of your presence.
  Kindle in all who are uncertain the gift of counsel.
  Kindle in all who are frightened the gift of tranquillity.
  Kindle in all who are in spiritual darkness the gift of light.

[Another single candle may be lighted from the Paschal candle followed by a brief period of quiet reflection. At the end of the period of silence, the presider or leader continues:]

Presider or Leader: The Spirit God gives is no rebellious spirit.
Assembly: Let us stir into flame the gift of God bestowed on us.

Presider or Leader: Let us pray as Jesus taught:
Assembly: Our Father . . .

Presider or Leader: Loving God, may the Spirit whom you send to be our Helper and Friend kindle in our hearts the fire of love. Keep your church attentive to the Spirit's voice that all peoples may be consoled by the light of truth. Grant this through Jesus Christ, our Redeemer, who lives and reigns with you and the Holy Spirit, one God forever and ever.

[The prayer may conclude with a blessing or in the absence of a priest or minister with the following:]

Presider or Leader: Let us bless our God
Assembly: And render thanks always. Amen.

Day Eight

[Presider or leader begins with the opening from page 216. The seven candles lighted on the previous days are lit from the beginning of the following prayer.]

Presider or Leader: Come, begetting Spirit who raised Jesus from the dead. Kindle in us the fire of your love.

Assembly:

Kindle in all who have lost faith the grace of conversion.

Kindle in all who struggle with sobriety the gift of strength.

Kindle in all who are scarred by abuse the gift of healing.

Kindle in all who cannot pray the gift of your help.

Kindle in all who are blind to God's love the gift of sight.

Kindle in all whose hearts are closed to love the gift of openness.

Kindle in all who persecute others the gift of sorrow.

Kindle in all who ridicule others the gift of contrition.

Kindle in all who are greedy the gift of generosity.

Kindle in all who are spiritually dead the gift of new life.

[Another single candle may be lighted from the Paschal candle followed by a brief period of quiet reflection. At the end of the period of silence, the presider or leader continues:]

Presider or Leader: The Spirit God gives is no merciless spirit.
Assembly: Let us stir into flame the gift of God bestowed on us.

Presider or Leader: Let us pray as Jesus taught:
Assembly: Our Father . . .

Presider or Leader: Loving God, may the Spirit whom you send to be our Helper and Friend kindle in our hearts the fire of love. Keep your church attentive to the Spirit's voice that all peoples may be consoled by the light of truth. Grant this through Jesus Christ, our Redeemer, who lives and reigns with you and the Holy Spirit, one God forever and ever.

[The prayer may conclude with a blessing or in the absence of a priest or minister with the following:]

Presider or Leader: Let us bless our God
Assembly: And render thanks always. Amen.

Day Nine

[Presider or leader begins with the opening from page 216. The eight candles lighted on the previous days are lit from the beginning of the following prayer.]

Presider or Leader: Come, anointing Spirit, fill the hearts of your faithful. Kindle in us the fire of your love.

Assembly:
Come, to all who wait on you in prayer.
Come, to those joined as one in the body of Christ through baptism.
Come, to those who feast on the Word of Life in the eucharistic banquet.
Come, to those who seek your pardon and peace as they confess their sins.
Come, to those whose faith in Christ has been sealed through confirmation.
Come, to those bound together in the covenant of marriage.
Come, to those consecrated to Christ and service to the church by ordination and religious vows.
Come, to the sick, aged, and infirmed who seek healing, comfort, and forgiveness.
Come, to those who sit in death's shadow awaiting the dawn of eternal light.

[The last candle may be lighted from the Paschal candle followed by a brief period of quiet reflection. At the end of the period of silence, the presider or leader continues:]

Gospel Proclamation: John 14:15-17

Presider or Leader: The Spirit God gives is no powerless spirit.
Assembly: Let us stir into flame the gift of God bestowed on us.

Presider or Leader: Lord, send out your Spirit
Assembly: And renew the face of the earth.

Presider or Leader: Let us pray as Jesus taught:
Assembly: Our Father . . .

Presider or Leader: Loving God, may the Spirit whom you send to be our Helper and Friend kindle in our hearts the fire of love. Keep your church attentive to the Spirit's voice that all peoples may be consoled by the light of truth. Grant this through Jesus Christ, our Redeemer, who lives and reigns with you and the Holy Spirit, one God forever and ever.

[The prayer may conclude with a blessing or in the absence of a priest or minister with the following:]

Presider or Leader: Let us bless our God
Assembly: And render thanks always. Amen.

Litany of the Holy Spirit

[Format #2, a novena of prayer for individual use]

[The following litany might be used as a novena of prayer in preparation for Pentecost. It could begin on the Friday after Ascension Day and conclude on Saturday, the vigil of Pentecost. It may also be used at other times throughout the year. The scripture reading should be prepared in advance. A single candle may be lighted before beginning the daily prayer.]

Day One

[The prayer begins with the Sign of the Cross.]

God, open my heart and mind to your word that I may be moved to prayer.

Scripture Reading: 2 Timothy 1:5-8a

Come, Holy Spirit, Gift of God most high. Kindle in us the fire of your love.
  Kindle in us the fire of reverence.
  Kindle in us the fire of nonviolence.
  Kindle in us the fire of tenderness.
  Kindle in us the fire of fidelity.
  Kindle in us the fire of humility.
  Kindle in us the fire of conversion.
  Kindle in us the fire of unceasing praise.
  Kindle in us the fire of persevering prayer.
  Kindle in us the fire of unfailing justice.
  Kindle in us the fire of generosity.

[A brief period of quiet reflection and personal prayer.]

The Spirit God gives is no cowardly spirit. Therefore, let us stir into flame the gift of God bestowed on us.

Our Father . . .

Concluding Prayer:
Loving God, may the Spirit whom you send to be our Helper and Friend kindle in our hearts the fire of love. Keep your church attentive to the Spirit's voice that all peoples may be consoled by the light of truth. Grant this through Jesus Christ, our Redeemer, who lives and reigns with you and the Holy Spirit, one God forever and ever.

Let us bless our God and render thanks always. Amen.

Day Two

[The prayer begins with the Sign of the Cross.]

God, open my heart and mind to your word that I may be moved to prayer.

Scripture Reading: Galatians 5:22-23a, 24-25

Come, Holy Spirit, Giver of Life. Kindle in us the fire of your love.
   Kindle in us the strength of the heart of Christ.
   Kindle in us the strength to proclaim the Truth.
   Kindle in us the strength to be chaste.
   Kindle in us the strength to live unselfishly.
   Kindle in us the strength to safeguard human freedom.
   Kindle in us the strength to stand with the economically poor.
   Kindle in us the strength to companion the dying.
   Kindle in us the strength to confront racism.
   Kindle in us the strength to confront sexism.
   Kindle in us the strength to bear wrongs patiently.

[A brief period of quiet reflection and personal prayer.]

The Spirit God gives is no listless spirit. Therefore, let us stir into flame the gift of God bestowed on us.

Our Father . . .

Concluding Prayer:
Loving God, may the Spirit whom you send to be our Helper and Friend kindle in our hearts the fire of love. Keep your church attentive to the Spirit's voice that all peoples may be consoled by the light of truth. Grant this through Jesus Christ, our Redeemer, who lives and reigns with you and the Holy Spirit, one God forever and ever.

Let us bless our God and render thanks always. Amen.

Day Three

[The prayer begins with the Sign of the Cross.]

God, open my heart and mind to your word that I may be moved to prayer.

Scripture Reading: Ephesians 1:3-4

Come, Holy Spirit, Giver of every good gift. Kindle in us the fire of your love.

Kindle in us the gift of faith.

Kindle in us the gift of hope.

Kindle in us the gift of discernment.

Kindle in us the gift of wonder.

Kindle in us the gift of healing.

Kindle in us the gift of listening.

Kindle in us the gift of joy.

Kindle in us the gift of respect for creation.

Kindle in us the gift of kindness.

Kindle in us the gift of surrender to God's will.

[A brief period of quiet reflection and personal prayer.]

The Spirit God gives is no hostile spirit. Therefore, let us stir into flame the gift of God bestowed on us.

Our Father . . .

Concluding Prayer:
Loving God, may the Spirit whom you send to be our Helper and Friend kindle in our hearts the fire of love. Keep your church attentive to the Spirit's voice that all peoples may be consoled by the light of truth. Grant this through Jesus Christ, our Redeemer, who lives and reigns with you and the Holy Spirit, one God forever and ever.

Let us bless our God and render thanks always. Amen.

Day Four

[The prayer begins with the Sign of the Cross.]

God, open my heart and mind to your word that I may be moved to prayer.

Scripture Reading: Titus 3:4-7

Come, Holy Spirit, Cause of our inspiration. Kindle in us the fire of your love.

Kindle in us holy boldness.

Kindle in us a sacred restlessness.

Kindle in us a desire for the greater gifts.

Kindle in us a passion for mercy.

Kindle in us an unfailing respect for life.

Kindle in us a love for simplicity.
Kindle in us a love for Wisdom.
Kindle in us a new Pentecost of peace.
Kindle in us a longing for the New Jerusalem.
Kindle in us the splendor of the Incarnate Word.

[A brief period of quiet reflection and personal prayer.]

The Spirit God gives is no unholy spirit. Therefore, let us stir into flame the gift of God bestowed on us.

Our Father . . .

Concluding Prayer:
Loving God, may the Spirit whom you send to be our Helper and Friend kindle in our hearts the fire of love. Keep your church attentive to the Spirit's voice that all peoples may be consoled by the light of truth. Grant this through Jesus Christ, our Redeemer, who lives and reigns with you and the Holy Spirit, one God forever and ever.

Let us bless our God and render thanks always. Amen.

Day Five

[The prayer begins with the Sign of the Cross.]

God, open my heart and mind to your word that I may be moved to prayer.

Scripture Reading: Romans 8:14-17

Come, Holy Spirit, source of our freedom. Kindle in us the fire of your love.
Kindle in us a freedom from fear.
Kindle in us a freedom from timidity.
Kindle in us a freedom from all jealousy.
Kindle in us a freedom to imagine.
Kindle in us a freedom to live with imperfections.
Kindle in us a freedom to embrace incompleteness in others.
Kindle in us a freedom from possessiveness.
Kindle in us a freedom to be in solidarity with the poor.
Kindle in us a freedom to let go of old hurts.
Kindle in us a freedom to move forward and not look back.

[A brief period of quiet reflection and personal prayer.]

The Spirit God gives is no oppressive spirit. Therefore, let us stir into flame the gift of God bestowed on us.

Our Father . . .

Concluding Prayer:
Loving God, may the Spirit whom you send to be our Helper and Friend kindle in our hearts the fire of love. Keep your church attentive to the Spirit's voice that all peoples may be consoled by the light of truth. Grant this through Jesus Christ, our Redeemer, who lives and reigns with you and the Holy Spirit, one God forever and ever.

Let us bless our God and render thanks always. Amen.

Day Six

[The prayer begins with the Sign of the Cross.]

God, open my heart and mind to your word that I may be moved to prayer.

Scripture Reading: 1 Corinthians 12:4-7

Come, sanctifying Spirit, our soul's delightful guest. Kindle in us the fire of your love.
Kindle in Pope [*Name*] the gift of holiness.
Kindle in all bishops the gift of love for your people.
Kindle in all priests the gift of selflessness.
Kindle in all deacons the gift of service.
Kindle in all religious the gift of fidelity.
Kindle in all theologians the gift of wisdom.
Kindle in all catechists the gift of knowledge.
Kindle in all lay ministers the gift of prayer.
Kindle in all missionaries the gift of zeal.
Kindle in all your people the gift of unity.

[A brief period of quiet reflection and personal prayer.]

The Spirit God gives is no arrogant spirit. Therefore, let us stir into flame the gift of God bestowed on us.

Our Father . . .

Concluding Prayer:

Loving God, may the Spirit whom you send to be our Helper and Friend kindle in our hearts the fire of love. Keep your church attentive to the Spirit's voice that all peoples may be consoled by the light of truth. Grant this through Jesus Christ, our Redeemer, who lives and reigns with you and the Holy Spirit, one God forever and ever.

Let us bless our God and render thanks always. Amen.

Day Seven

[The prayer begins with the Sign of the Cross.]

God, open my heart and mind to your word that I may be moved to prayer.

Scripture Reading: Ephesians 4:1-3

Come, consoling Spirit, Light Divine. Kindle in us the fire of your love.
  Kindle in all spouses the gift of fidelity.
  Kindle in all families the gift of peace.
  Kindle in all parents the gift of tenderness.
  Kindle in all children the gift of respect.
  Kindle in all who grieve the gift of consolation.
  Kindle in all who are engaged the gift of discernment.
  Kindle in all who are lonely the gift of your presence.
  Kindle in all who are uncertain the gift of counsel.
  Kindle in all who are frightened the gift of tranquillity.
  Kindle in all who are in spiritual darkness the gift of light.

[A brief period of quiet reflection and personal prayer.]

The Spirit God gives is no rebellious spirit. Therefore, let us stir into flame the gift of God bestowed on us.

Our Father . . .

Concluding Prayer:

Loving God, may the Spirit whom you send to be our Helper and Friend kindle in our hearts the fire of love. Keep your church attentive to the Spirit's voice that all peoples may be consoled by the light of truth. Grant this through Jesus Christ, our Redeemer, who lives and reigns with you and the Holy Spirit, one God forever and ever.

Let us bless our God and render thanks always. Amen.

Day Eight

[The prayer begins with the Sign of the Cross.]

God, open my heart and mind to your word that I may be moved to prayer.

Scripture Reading: Romans 8:26-27

Come, begetting Spirit who raised Jesus from the dead. Kindle in us the fire of your love.
  Kindle in all who have lost faith the grace of conversion.
  Kindle in all who struggle with sobriety the gift of strength.
  Kindle in all who are scarred by abuse the gift of healing.
  Kindle in all who cannot pray the gift of your help.
  Kindle in all who are blind to God's love the gift of sight.
  Kindle in all whose hearts are closed to love the gift of openness.
  Kindle in all who persecute others the gift of sorrow.
  Kindle in all who ridicule others the gift of contrition.
  Kindle in all who are greedy the gift of generosity.
  Kindle in all who are spiritually dead the gift of new life.

[A brief period of quiet reflection and personal prayer.]

The Spirit God gives is no merciless spirit. Therefore, let us stir into flame the gift of God bestowed on us.

Our Father . . .

Concluding Prayer:
Loving God, may the Spirit whom you send to be our Helper and Friend kindle in our hearts the fire of love. Keep your church attentive to the Spirit's voice that all peoples may be consoled by the light of truth. Grant this through Jesus Christ, our Redeemer, who lives and reigns with you and the Holy Spirit, one God forever and ever.

Let us bless our God and render thanks always. Amen.

Day Nine

[The prayer begins with the Sign of the Cross.]

God, open my heart and mind to your word that I may be moved to prayer.

Scripture Reading: 1 Corinthians 12:12-13

Come, anointing Spirit, fill the hearts of your faithful. Kindle in us the fire of your love.

Come, to all who wait on you in prayer.

Come, to those joined as one in the body of Christ through baptism.

Come, to those who feast on the Word of Life in the eucharistic banquet.

Come, to those who seek your pardon and peace as they confess their sins.

Come, to those whose faith in Christ has been sealed through confirmation.

Come, to those bound together in the covenant of marriage.

Come, to those consecrated to Christ and service to the church by ordination and religious vows.

Come, to the sick, aged, and infirmed who seek healing, comfort, and forgiveness.

Come, to those who sit in death's shadow awaiting the dawn of eternal light.

[A brief period of quiet reflection and personal prayer.]

Gospel Reading: John 14:15-17

The Spirit God gives is no powerless spirit. Therefore, let us stir into flame the gift of God bestowed on us.

Lord, send out your Spirit and renew the face of the earth.

Our Father . . .

Concluding Prayer:
Loving God, may the Spirit whom you send to be our Helper and Friend kindle in our hearts the fire of love. Keep your church attentive to the Spirit's voice that all peoples may be consoled by the light of truth. Grant this through Jesus Christ, our Redeemer, who lives and reigns with you and the Holy Spirit, one God forever and ever.

Let us bless our God and render thanks always. Amen.

Litany for Peace
Option #1

[The following litany may be used in common or private. The prayer begins with the Sign of the Cross.]

Leader: Come, Holy Spirit, fill the hearts of your faithful.
All: Kindle in us your peace.
Leader: Come, enlightening Spirit, open our hearts to receive good news.
All: And by the beauty of God's word, living and true, renew the face of the earth.
~~Scripture Reading:~~ Philippians 4:6-8, 9b

Leader: Let us summon the Spirit for our consolation.
All: Spirit, our Consoler, may we be at peace! [Repeat after each petition.]

With situations we must learn to accept without the reconciliation between
persons . . .
With departures of friends and loved ones without farewell . . .
With diminished energy in our bodies . . .
With illness beyond our power to heal . . .

With enforced retirement . . .
With unjustifiable termination of employment . . .
With those who betrayed our trust . . .
With ourselves when we betrayed someone's trust . . .

With the regrets we carry within us . . .
With lost opportunities to be a healing presence . . .
With stances we could have taken but did not . . .
With changes that are not to our liking . . .

With disappointments that were hard to accept . . .
With dreams that have not materialized . . .

Leader: Let us pray for a greater openness to the gifts of grace.
All: Spirit, empower us anew! [Repeat after each petition.]

To be reverent despite human short-comings . . .
To be kind instead of harsh or critical . . .
To be joyful in sharing others' blessings . . .
To be wise in discerning opportunities for doing good . . .

To be wonder-filled at our personal giftedness . . .
 To be sensitive to the woundedness of others . . .
To be strong so as to carry others' burdens . . .
 To be courageous in facing the future . . .

To be honest and humble with our limitations . . .
 To be faith-filled despite our losses . . .
To be hope-filled as we see our life passing away . . .
 To be loving so as to share in God's transformation of our world . . .

[Any spontaneous petitions, intercessions, or prayers of gratitude may be included here, or a period of quiet reflection for personal prayer.]

Leader: Let us bring our prayer to a close.

Concluding Prayer: "God of Our Journey"

> God of our journey,
> Source of our life,
> Word of Redemption,
> Fire and Light.
> Whisper and Wind-song
> Sun and our shade,
> Water, oasis,
> North-star of night.
>
> O God of our journey
> Beginning and end,
> Sustainer of pilgrims,
> Protector and guide,
> Mother who nurtures,
> Father who cares,
> Sister companion,
> Brother beside.
>
> Weaver of dreams,
> Fulfill our hopes:
> Be dawn after darkness
> and strength in our fight.
> Raincloud of Mercy
> in our deserts of pain,
> Be our certain tomorrow
> when we pass through death's night. Amen.

Litany for Peace
Option #2, Entrusting the Past Year to God

[This prayer service is suitable for an end of the year day of prayer or retreat. The leader begins by greeting those present and inviting the assembly into prayerful reflection. The format presented here involves numerous voices. It may be adapted to the circumstances.]

Leader:

The passing of seasons brings change. The years contain losses and gains. Some faces that were part of our landscape have gone, not to be replaced. New faces and personalities come into our lives, and we're challenged to make a home for a stranger. We are reminded again and again that life moves on and we cannot turn back.

Voice 1:

Our longings go in both directions. We memorialize the past in pictures, trophies, the pages of our journals and scrapbooks, in our necrology and cemeteries, and mostly in our hearts. We look to the future not knowing who or what will emerge or when. The future invites our hope while it also calls us to wait, sometimes in silence, sometimes alone.

Voice 2:

We watch the face of families and community change: new life or new spouses whose names we must learn, new neighbors whose ways are different from the last ones, new colleagues with unique gifts and personalities, some who are too young to recall the "old days," new leaders with styles of their own, new ways of approaching timeless issues, new policies to replace those once "carved in stone," new challenges to be addressed with limited resources, new expectations placed upon the young.

Voice 3:

We watch our bodies change: less energy for some of the old folks, loss of memory where there once was a vibrant mind, a cane to sturdy faltering steps, a quiver in the voice, slower reflexes, failing eyesight, loss of appetite, less resilience.

Voice 4:

New fears come with age: the ice and cold, the traffic, the cost of living on fixed incomes, the loss of control and independence, the fear of being sidelined by a younger generation, the inability to cope with continuous change or to protect oneself, the possibility of being left alone or a debilitating illness. Even the reality of death can bring on fear.

Voice 5:
Time makes us wonder about many things: an old childhood friend, a lost relative, former colleagues, students, or classmates, the family that left the parish, the sixth-grade teacher, a resigned priest we've not seen again, the pen-pal we never met, the nurse who was so gentle, the old neighbors who moved away, the prayers that were not answered to our expectation, the choices we made when we were younger, the battles we won and the wars we lost.

Leader: Will we recover from our losses? Heal from our wounds? Arrive at forgiveness? Achieve the goals we set?

Where are we going? Where have we been? In particular, where has this year's journey taken us, individually and communally?

Quiet Reflection [Reflective, instrumental music may be used here.]

A Litany for Peace

Leader: Let us summon the Spirit for our consolation.
All: Spirit, our Consoler, may we be at peace! [Repeat after each petition.]

With situations we must learn to accept without the reconciliation between
          persons . . .
     With departures of friends and loved ones without farewell . . .
With diminished energy in our bodies . . .
     With illness beyond our power to heal . . .

With enforced retirement . . .
     With unjustifiable termination of employment . . .
With those who betrayed our trust . . .
     With ourselves when we betrayed someone's trust . . .

With the regrets we carry within us . . .
     With lost opportunities to be a healing presence . . .
With stances we could have taken but did not . . .
     With changes that are not to our liking . . .

With disappointments that were hard to accept . . .
     With dreams that have not materialized . . .

Leader: Let us pray for a greater openness to the gifts of grace.
All: Spirit, empower us anew! [Repeat after each petition.]

To be reverent despite human short-comings . . .
     To be kind instead of harsh or critical . . .

To be joyful in sharing others' blessings . . .
　　To be wise in discerning opportunities for doing good . . .

To be wonder-filled at our personal giftedness . . .
　　To be sensitive to the woundedness of others . . .

To be strong so as to carry others' burdens . . .
　　To be courageous in facing the future . . .

To be honest and humble with our limitations . . .
　　To be faith-filled despite our losses . . .

To be hope-filled as we see our life passing away . . .
　　To be loving so as to share in God's transformation of our world . . .

[The assembly may be invited to offer spontaneous petitions or prayers of gratitude.]

Concluding Prayer: "God of Our Journey"

> God of our journey,
> Source of our life,
> Word of Redemption,
> Fire and Light.
> Whisper and Wind-song
> Sun and our shade,
> Water, oasis,
> North-star of night.
>
> O God of our journey
> Beginning and end,
> Sustainer of pilgrims,
> Protector and guide,
> Mother who nurtures,
> Father who cares,
> Sister companion,
> Brother beside.
>
> Weaver of dreams,
> Fulfill our hopes:
> Be dawn after darkness
> and strength in our fight.
> Raincloud of Mercy
> in our deserts of pain,
> Be our certain tomorrow
> when we pass through death's night.

[The presider may bring the prayer service to a close with a Prayer Over the People taken from the Roman Sacramentary.]

Presider: Let us go trusting in God's Word and Spirit to guide and sustain us.
Assembly: Thanks be to God.

Commemoration of the Dead

[This service is appropriate during the month of November when the church prays for the faithful departed. The Easter candle is lighted and placed in a prominent position. A bowl of incense may also be used in this service. When incense is used the assembly might be invited to mention aloud the names of deceased persons they wish to have remembered. This would occur as the presider or other minister sprinkles incense on the coals.]

Presider: The grace and peace of God, the love of Jesus and the consoling Spirit be with you.

Presider: Redeeming God, let our prayer rise like incense to you.
Assembly: Hear the sound of our pleading.

Presider: Show us your mercy and love.
Assembly: Grant us your salvation.

[The presider or another minister begins sprinkling incense on the coals, saying:]

Sisters and brothers, let us remember aloud the names of those whose memory we carry in our hearts this day/evening and whom we wish to commend to the mercy of God.

[When the assembly has been given sufficient opportunity to do so, the presider continues.]

Presider: In faith we turn to God, who is all compassionate and judges with fairness and equity. God alone can read the depths of human hearts. Only God knows the faith and trust of people. In prayer now we ask God to fulfill for all the dead the promise of mercy announced to Abraham and Sarah and fulfilled in Christ.

Scripture Reading: Sirach 18:1-3, 8-13 [Some other scriptural text, other than a gospel, may be used. An appropriate hymn, preferably a psalm, may follow the reading.]

A Litany for the Dead

Presider: Let us pray.

Presider: For those who have died alone without consolation of family or friends:
Assembly: Remember your consoling love, O Christ!

Presider: For those who met death by violence:
Assembly: Remember your violent death, O Christ!

Presider: For those who died in the cause of peace:

Assembly: Remember how hatred called for your death, O Christ!

Presider: For those who have died as a result of hunger and thirst:

Assembly: Remember how you were thirsty at the hour of your death, O Christ!

Presider: For those who have died in the service of your gospel:

Assembly: Remember your promise, O Christ, that your servants shall not want.

Presider: For those who have died from lack of love, especially infants and children:

Assembly: Remember, O Christ, that to these belong the reign of heaven!

Presider: For those who have died in fires because of poor housing and neglect:

Assembly: Remember, O Christ, that in the bosom of Abraham, Lazarus is no longer poor!

Presider: For those who have died as innocent civilians caught in the midst of war:

Assembly: Remember, O Christ, you were the innocent Lamb slain for the guilty!

Presider: For those who have fallen victim to racial, ethnic, religious, and gender discrimination:

Assembly: Remember, O Christ, your promise to be the Good Shepherd of the flock!

Presider: For those who have died as martyrs of justice and compassion:

Assembly: Remember, O Christ, the blessedness promised to those persecuted for what is right and just!

Presider: For those who have died as a result of their own despair and loneliness:

Assembly: Remember, O Christ, those who stand in most need of your mercy!

Presider: For those who have died because of their addictions:

Assembly: Remember, O Christ, your love alone transforms our worst failings into a future where every tear is wiped away!

Presider: For those who have died with no belief in eternity:

Assembly: Remember, O Christ, your passion embraced the universe!

Presider: For our parents and relatives:
Assembly: God, save your people!

Presider: For our sisters and brothers: in our birth families, parishes, and religious congregations:
Assembly: God, grant us salvation!

Presider: For those we have known as friends, spouses, or life companions:
Assembly: Come, O Christ, with plenteous redemption!

Presider: Eternal rest grant to them, O Christ!
Assembly: Let everlasting light shine on them!

The Gospel Proclamation: John 6:37-40

[Another appropriate gospel text may be used.]

Presider's Prayer:
Compassionate God, Source of forgiveness and salvation for all humanity, hear our prayers for those who have gone from this life. Receive with tender mercy those who come to you in the humility and brokenness of their lives. Cleanse them of sin through the death of Jesus that all may rise at your word to the glory of the resurrection. We ask this in the name of Jesus, our Resurrection and Life, who lives and reigns with you and the Holy Spirit, one God, forever and ever.

[The service may conclude with a blessing which occurs in the customary manner. The presider or another minister dismisses the assembly:]

Our prayer is ended. Let us go peace.

[An appropriate hymn, such as "Salve Regina," may be sung.]